SpringerBriefs in Law

More information about this series at http://www.springer.com/series/10164

Markku Suksi

Double Enumeration of Legislative Powers in a Sub-State Context

A Comparison between Canada, Denmark and Finland

Springer

Markku Suksi
Department of Law
Åbo Akademi University
Turku
Finland

ISSN 2192-855X ISSN 2192-8568 (electronic)
SpringerBriefs in Law
ISBN 978-3-319-90920-2 ISBN 978-3-319-90921-9 (eBook)
https://doi.org/10.1007/978-3-319-90921-9

Library of Congress Control Number: 2018940879

Printed on acid-free paper

This Springer imprint is published by the registered company Springer International Publishing AG part of Springer Nature
The registered company address is: Gewerbestrasse 11, 6330 Cham, Switzerland

Preface

The research for this book was made possible by a sabbatical for research provided by my university, Åbo Akademi University in Finland, in collaboration with the pool of professors in Finland and Svenska kulturfonden. I am grateful to these funders and also to Director John Packer of the Human Rights Research and Education Center at the University of Ottawa, Canada, for hosting me in October and November 2015. I also wish to thank Mr. Sjúrður Rasmussen, Legal Expert to the Legislative Assembly of the Faroe Islands and Professor Pierre Foucher of the University of Ottawa Law School for materials and comments. I am grateful to Mrs. Anna Barlow, Barrister, BA, MA, for linguistic and editorial comments and to Springer-Verlag for publishing my research. All the errors that may remain in the text are entirely my responsibility.

As concerns the Åland Islands, this book relies in part on previous research, *inter alia*, Markku Suksi, *Sub-State Governance through Territorial Autonomy*, published by Springer-Verlag in 2011. The normative materials included in the research reflect the situation at the end of 2017.

Turku/Åbo, Finland
March 2018

Markku Suksi

Contents

List of Cases and Opinions

Canada

Denmark

Færøernes Landsstyrelse og Heilsumálaráðið mod Region Hovedstaden, Danmarks Højesterets dom 3. juni 2016, 1. afd., sag 160/2015, *p. 54.*
Føroya Landsstýri mod Karsten Werner Larsen, Ø.L.D., Østre Landsrets dom 5. juli 1983 i anke 5-295/1982, *p. 54.*
Henrik Weihe Joensen mod Fiskimálaráðið, Sorinskrivarin I Føroyum, 2. maj 2016, sag nr. BS 899/2015, *pp. 55, 56.*

Finland

Supreme Administrative Court, decision 1982-A-II-1 (mutual exclusivity of legal orders), *p. 38.*
Supreme Administrative Court, decision 2003:1 (inapplicability of national law in Åland), *p. 38.*
Administrative Court of the Åland Islands of 15 November 2017, No. 80/2017 (conveyance tax on incorporated municipal harbor in Åland), *p. 51.*
Supreme Court, decision 1993:90 (determination of administrative competence), *p. 52.*
Supreme Court, decision 1998:8 (determination of administrative competence), *p. 52.*
Supreme Court, decision 2001:38 (determination of administrative competence), *p. 52.*
Supreme Court, decision 2001:79 (Parliament's competence in lotteries law), *p. 50.*
Supreme Court, decision 2004:65 (salmon fishing quotas an EU competence), *p. 40.*
Supreme Court, decision 2005:27 (marketing of Ålandic lotteries in mainland Finland), *p. 50.*
Supreme Court, decision 2005:87 (public order and security a competence of Åland), *p. 51.*
Supreme Court, decision 2017:47 (determination of administrative competence for fishing quota without agreement), *pp. 40, 52.*
Supreme Court, decision 2017:48 (determination of administrative competence), *p. 52.*
Supreme Court, decision 2018:16 (length of driving prohibition), *pp. 51, 52.*
Turku Court of Appeals of 10 January 2017 (R16/1828) (length of driving prohibition), *p. 52.*
Opinion of the Supreme Court of 5 April 1963 (quantity of national law in Ålandic law), *p. 73.*
Opinion of the Supreme Court of 19 June 1979 (early watertight compartments thinking), *p. 69.*
Opinion of the Supreme Court, 9 September 1994, Nr 3169 (Dnr OH 94/104; advisory EU referendum), *p. 88.*
Opinion of the Supreme Court of 21 March 1996 (gene technology), *p. 90.*

Court of Justice of the European Union

Costa v. Enel, 15 July 1964, Case 6/641 [1], *pp. 95, 98.*

European Court of Human Rights

Ekholm v. Finland, Application no. 68050/01, European Court of Human Rights, Judgment of 24 July 2007, *p. 33.*

United Nations Human Rights Committee

Ballantyne, Davidson, McIntyre v. Canada, Communications Nos. 359/1989 and 385/1989 to the UN Human Rights Committee, U.N. Doc. CCPR/C/47/D/359/1989 and 385/1989/Rev.1 (1993), *p. 33.*
Waldman v. Canada, Communication No 694/1996 to the UN Human Rights Committee, meeting of 3 November 1999, U.N.Doc. CCPR/C/67/D/694/1996, *p. 33.*

Chapter 1
Introduction

Canada is an unusual federation in relation to its federal units, the provinces, just as Denmark and Finland are unusual unitary states in relation to those self-governing or autonomous entities that are part of their constitutional fabric (the Faroe Islands and the Åland Islands, respectively).[1]

In a regular federation, the distribution of legislative powers between the federation and the states is normally arranged so that the federal legislature has enumerated powers, while the states are in the possession of so-called residual powers, perhaps as a reminder of their original sovereignty as states before being incorporated into the federation.[2] This is not so in Canada, where the legislative powers of both the federal level and the provinces are enumerated in lists of law-making powers that in principle are meant to be exclusive in relation to each other. In fact, Canada has sometimes been characterised as quasi-federal.[3]

For a typical autonomy arrangement embedded in a unitary state, the situation is often the reverse: the parliament of the country, which in principle is a unitary state, functions on the basis of residual powers, while the autonomous entity has enumerated powers, granted either under the constitution of the country or by dele-

---

[1]The distribution of legislative powers between the Danish Parliament and the Legislative Assembly of Greenland is organized in a manner that comes close to the solution concerning the Faroe Islands, but does not entail any enumeration of powers for the Danish Parliament and allows the Greenlandic legislature to transfer by its own decisions law-making powers from Denmark to Greenland for the purposes of legislating for Greenland. In fact, in the 2009 Self-Government Act concerning Greenland, the Danish Parliament went so far as to make possible the transfer of all legislative areas to Greenland and the declaration of independence by Greenland.

[2]In principle (although some variations of the theme exist), this seems to be so, for instance, in the United States, Australia, Switzerland, Germany (with a list of concurrent powers), and Austria, supported by a supremacy clause or a principle of federal preemption. The distribution of powers in Belgium seems to be a further variation of this theme, and in Switzerland, too, the cantons are in the possession of an original sovereignty and residuality in legislative powers, although the Swiss constitution actually lands in an enumeration of both the federal and the cantonal powers, subject to the provision that federal law takes precedence over cantonal law.

[3]See Wheare 1964, p. 19. See also Inwood 2013, pp. 108, 264–267.

M. Suksi, *Double Enumeration of Legislative Powers in a Sub-State Context*, SpringerBriefs in Law, https://doi.org/10.1007/978-3-319-90921-9_1

gation under ordinary legislation of that country. This is not so in Denmark for the Faroe Islands or in Finland for the Åland Islands, where the legislative powers of not only the legislative assemblies of the autonomies but also the national parliaments are enumerated. In Denmark, the position of the Faroe Islands (and Greenland) in relation to Denmark proper is often characterized in terms of a commonwealth, while in Finland, the Åland Islands has a *sui generis* status typical of a number of other autonomous territories in the world.

The overall picture shows that amongst the approximately 100 countries in the world that are either federally organized or that contain an autonomy arrangement, there exist a number of states where the distribution of legislative powers is organized in an atypical manner by double enumeration. In contrast to single enumerations found in regular federations or states with autonomy arrangements, double enumerations are specific enough to warrant a study of these constitutional arrangements as a separate contingent.[4] The focus of this research is therefore on the issue of double enumeration of legislative powers, as the distribution of powers with single enumeration in federal settings and for more regular autonomy arrangements has been amply dealt with in other research.[5] Constitutional systems which organize the distribution of legislative powers in a sub-state setting along two lists of enumerations, one for the national level and another for the sub-state level, are likely to feature interesting similarities and differences with respect to a host of issues:[6] what are the (historical) reasons for the explicit duality? How exclusive are the two lists of enumerations, that is, can either of the competences under some

---

[4]Other examples that could be mentioned is the relationship between mainland China, on the one hand, and Hong Kong and Macau, on the other. See Suksi 2011, pp. 279–295. Also the relationship between France and New Caledonia is fashioned in this way, at least until October 2018, when a referendum on the possible independence of New Caledonia is due to be held. On New Caledonia, see David 2008. In India, both the Union and the states exercise their legislative powers on the basis of their respective exclusive enumerations of legislative competences and both orders of government on the basis of a listing of concurrent powers, but the federation or the centre nonetheless seems to be in the possession of the residual powers and relatively far-reaching supremacy. These features make India more like an ordinary federation, but with certain unitary features, except for the state of Jammu and Kashmir, which has a particular position in the Indian federation. It could be argued that the Indian distribution of powers should also be dealt with in this analysis, but for reasons of space, India will be excluded here, although might be analysed at some further point of time in another piece of research.

[5]On distribution of powers in federal settings, see, e.g., Watts 2008 and Anderson 2008. On distribution of powers in autonomy settings, see, e.g., Benedikter 2007 and Suksi 2011.

[6]A similar distinction between double and single enumeration is made in Craig and Walters 2000, pp. 233–236, where Canada is mentioned as the sole example of double enumeration, while Australia is mentioned as a current example of single enumeration. In fact, Craig and Walters divide single enumeration into two variants, one of residuality at the sub-state level (Australia) and another of restriction from legislating in relation to a list of reserved matters (Scotland). See also Craig and Walters 2000, p. 239: "The choice between the Canadian and Australian approaches is therefore dependent upon a political choice about the right balance to strike between legislatures…", but in interpretations of competence issues, the approaches from both may be instructive (although it appears as if the Canadian example might be somewhat less useful in the context of competence adjudication on the basis of the Scotland Act).

conditions override the other side's legislative decisions? How is duality in the distribution of legislative powers managed, for instance, from the point of view of a supremacy doctrine or an acceptance of potentially concurrent powers? Which are the consequences of this duality, for instance, in relation to matters that emerge with the development of society and which have not been explicitly enumerated?

To answer these research questions and to indicate that there is a middle position between single enumerations in a regular federal-like and a regular autonomy-like distribution of legislative powers, the legislation in the three countries (Canada, Denmark and Finland) establishing separate enumerations for the national level and the sub-state level is studied. That legislation is identified in the next chapter. In addition, the interpretation of the competence line based on double enumeration between the national parliament and the sub-state entities is carried out, where relevant, on the basis of *travaux preparatoires* of the fundamental norms on which the arrangements are based, judicial or quasi-judicial resolutions of competence problems, and relevant doctrine and literature.

This piece approaches a particular constitutional issue, the distribution of legislative powers, from a comparative perspective with the aim of introducing this category of distribution of legislative powers to a wider audience. At the same time, however, this research is a contribution to the discussion on divided sovereignty, that is, to a more legal-theoretical problem of how and where law can be made and under which conditions. This is also the reason that the issue of size of the various jurisdictions involved is not considered: the theoretical and legal problems are assumed to be similar irrespective of the size of the countries or the sub-state jurisdictions involved. More specifically, the question is how it is possible to split the legal order into two material spheres that are exclusive to each other so that each legislator knows, at least by and large, its own area of competence and how possible competence problems are adjudicated. This piece also aims to contribute to the understanding of how sub-state solutions can be designed by indicating a middle ground between a typical federation and a typical autonomy arrangement. The intention is to provide some reference points for countries such as the United Kingdom, where devolution of law-making powers is a constant constitutional issue, and to inform debates concerning sub-state solutions elsewhere in the world. This piece may also be seen as a contribution to the ongoing debate concerning the distribution of legislative competence between the European Union and its Member States.

This research does not cover several other interesting issues related to the exercise of law-making powers in federations and autonomy arrangements, such as the observance of the constitutional rights of individuals and the amendment of the fundamental norms establishing the rules of distribution of powers. The exercise of treaty powers and participation of the relevant sub-state entities in foreign affairs is dealt with in certain relevant contexts, but is not systematically covered as a cross-cutting theme.

References

Anderson G (2008) Federalism: an introduction. Oxford University Press, Oxford

Benedikter T (2007) The world's working regional autonomies: an introduction and comparative analysis. Anthem Press, London, New York, Delhi

Craig P, Walters M (2000) The courts, devolution and judicial review. In: Forsyth C (ed) Judicial review and the constitution. Hart Publishing, Oxford and Portland, Oregon, pp 213–244

David CG (2008) Essai sur la loi du pays calédonienne. L'Harmattan, Paris

Inwood GJ (2013) Understanding Canadian Federalism—an introduction to theory and practice. Pearson, Toronto

Suksi M (2011) Sub-state governance through territorial autonomy. Springer, Heidelberg

Watts RL (2008) Comparing federal systems. McGill-Queen's University Press, Toronto

Wheare KC (1964) Federal government, 4th edn. Oxford University Press, New York

Chapter 2
Construction of Two Enumerations

2.1 Constitutional Basis

In the Canadian Constitution, the Constitution Act 1867,[1] the principal enumeration of competences for the two law-making spheres is established in Section 91 on the powers of the Parliament and Section 92 on the exclusive powers of the provincial legislatures. Interestingly, the enumerations of the powers of the federation and of the provinces are defined as exclusive in the opening paragraph of each Section. However, there is an indication of some residuality attached to the federal powers in the opening paragraph of Section 91 by means of the grant to the federation of powers to make laws for the entire country for the peace, order and good government (hereinafter: the POGG) in relation to all matters not coming within the classes of subjects assigned exclusively to the legislatures of the provinces. This partial and—as we shall see—limited residuality for the federal law-maker is yet another indication of the unusual construction of the Canadian federalism when compared with other federations; one would normally expect to find residuality at the sub-state level in federations.

The situation is similar concerning the Åland Islands. Section 75(2) of the 2000 Constitution of Finland makes reference to the fact that the Åland Islands have legislative powers, but Section 75 and Section 120, in particular, depart from the idea that there is a separate piece of law that establish the modalities of the self-government or autonomy of the Åland Islands. The recognition of the principle that two legislators exist within the Finnish constitutional order carried through to the 1991 Self-Government Act of Åland,[2] which establishes two lists of legislative powers, one for the national parliament in Section 27 and another for the Legislative Assembly of the Åland Islands in Section 18. The starting point with

[1]For the Constitution Act, 1867, see http://laws-lois.justice.gc.ca/eng/Const//index.html#docCont (accessed on 4 January 2018).
[2]For a translation into English of the 1991 Self-Government Act, see http://www.finlex.fi/fi/laki/kaannokset/1991/en19911144.pdf (accessed on 4 January 2018).

M. Suksi, *Double Enumeration of Legislative Powers in a Sub-State Context*, SpringerBriefs in Law, https://doi.org/10.1007/978-3-319-90921-9_2

the two enumerations is to establish decisively the distribution of legislative powers for the jurisdiction of Åland. In some matters, the Parliament of Finland is competent to legislate for the Åland Islands, meaning that Åland is not exempted from the application of the national law in these fields of law, while in some other matters, the Legislative Assembly of the Åland Islands is competent to legislate for the Åland Islands, meaning that the jurisdiction of Åland is exempted from the application of national law in those fields of law, where the legislator of the Åland Islands may enact law or may refrain from enacting law (in which case national law shall not gain applicability so as to fill the normative vacuum). This constitutional arrangement is established by the 1991 Self-Government Act, which is itself not part of the formal Constitution, despite being clearly of a constitutional nature as, for instance, it can only be amended by the same method as the Constitution and by the consent of the Legislative Assembly of Åland.

For the Faroe Islands, no provisions on the distribution of legislative powers exist in the Danish Constitution. This is curious because the autonomy arrangement was instituted as early as 1948 by ordinary legislation and it could have been taken into account and recognized when the Constitution of Denmark was enacted in 1953, by means of inserting explicit provisions on the autonomy of the Faroe Islands.[3] However, the four provisions in the Danish Constitution concerning the Faroe Islands deal with the allocation of two seats of the Danish Parliament to the Faroe Islands and with the organization of elections in the Faroe Islands without any bearing on the distribution of legislative powers. Perhaps the arrangement is now best described as one based on customary constitutional law or on constitutional convention. In any event, the legislative powers of the Faroe Islands, first identified in the 1948 Home Rule Act,[4] are today supplemented by the provisions in the 2005 Act on the Transfer of Legislative Powers (hereinafter: the Takeover Act),[5] both of which are pieces of ordinary law enacted by means of simple majority in the Danish Parliament.

The latter act amends the former by making it possible for the Faroese legislative assembly to transfer, by its own legislative decisions, legislative powers from the Danish Parliament and add them to those powers that the Legislative Assembly of the Faroe Islands already has either on the basis of explicit reference in the 1948 Act or on the basis of earlier transfer decisions. This means that an enumeration of legislative powers of the Faroe Islands is emerging in a piecemeal manner, but is of

---

[3]At the material time, the understanding seemed to be that the self-government of the Faroe Islands was of a delegated nature, to some extent comparable to municipalities, but over the decades, the arrangement is increasingly understood as one where the different parts of Denmark constitute a Commonwealth under the Constitution of Denmark where the Legislative Assembly of the Faroe Islands exercises legislative powers proper. See Sølvará 2003, pp. 168–175.

[4]Lov nr. 137 af 23. Marts 1948 om Færøernes Hjemmestyre, or the so-called 1948 Home Rule Act, available in translation into English at http://stm.dk/_p_13089.html (accessed on 4 January 2018).

[5]Lov nr. 578 af 24. Juni 2005 om de færøske myndigheders overtagelse af sager og sagsområder, or the so-called 2005 Takeover Act, available in translation into English at http://stm.dk/_p_13089.html (accessed on 4 January 2018).

a more fragmentary nature than any explicit listing in a constitution or comparable act: the various separate transfer decisions can, taken together, be understood as such an enumeration. At the same time, the situation is exceptional in that the sub-state entity can by its own decision take over legislative powers from the national law-maker. There is, however, a limit to this power, as Section 1(2) of the 2005 Act prohibits the transfer of a small number of enumerated matters, leaving them in the hands of the Danish Parliament. With that limitation by means of the listed matters, an enumeration is also established for the national law-maker. Hence in principle, both law-makers are operating on the basis of an enumeration, although current practice on the part of the Faroe Islands display characteristics that could be said to deviate from this general proposition in a more federal direction.

2.2 Legislative History Behind Two Lists of Enumerations

Historically, the American War of Independence against the British may have been the direct reason that Britain, after taking over the French possessions in what is now Canada in 1763, needed to create an administrative solution for the remaining British territories in North America: the area needed to be kept peaceful and positive to the British.[6] The adoption of the Quebec Act by the British Parliament in 1774 recognised the validity of French law, the French language and the Catholic religion in the region and brought to an end the assimilationist policies implemented during the previous decade. The creation of two entities in the British territories, Lower Canada (i.e., Quebec) and Upper Canada (i.e., Ontario), was in 1840 turned into a broader territorial configuration, which failed to produce a viable jurisdiction, perhaps mainly because of a lack of responsible government and an inability to accommodate the French language and the concerns of French-speakers.[7] After a period of deliberation, with a meeting in Charlottetown in 1864 (where the general idea of a federal constitution was presented) and in Quebec City in 1864 (where the principles were worked out) as well as a constitutional convention in London in 1866 (where the details were developed), a new entity was finally created under the

[6]More specifically on the various reasons for the evolution of the pre-Confederation Canada, see Inwood 2013, pp. 24–45.

[7]See Hogg 2014, who emphasizes the French language and the Catholic religion in the context [NB! References to Hogg 2014 are to sections in the supplemented loose-leaf volume, not to pages]. See also Inwood 2013, pp. 45–55, and Smith 2010, pp. 40–61. In the scheme of distribution of legislative competence in Canada, language is ancillary to a main legislative competence. The order of government that that has law-making power over courts has the power to decide the language of courts (*Jones v. A.G. of New Brunswick*, [1975] 2 SCR 182, 1974 CanLII 164 (SCC); provincial and also some federal power) and the one that has law-making power over commerce also has jurisdiction over language of commerce or various materials produced by business operations (*Devine v. Quebec (Attorney General)*, [1988] 2 SCR 790, 1988 CanLII 20 (SCC); provincial power), but when passing such laws, the linguistic rights of the Constitution must be respected and taken into account.

British North America Act of 1867 (the BNA), enacted by the Parliament of England, that included not only Quebec and Ontario as separate provinces, but also other parts of the colony.

The BNA, also referred to as the Constitution Act, 1867, created the Dominion of Canada as a "confederation" which could already at that stage be described as federal in its organisation, with the division of law-making competences described above. The confederation was later joined by other provinces, as the sub-state entities are termed in Canada. Today, Canada consists of ten provinces (Alberta, British Columbia, Manitoba, New Brunswick, Newfoundland and Labrador, Nova Scotia, Ontario, Prince Edward Island, Quebec, and Saskatchewan) and of three territories (Northwest Territories, Nunavut, and Yukon). Nunavut has an autonomy arrangement distinguishable from a federal relationship, governed under the 1999 Nunavut Act, enacted by the federal Parliament.[8] In addition to the provinces, the territories have also been granted a seat in the senate.

The British North America Act was amended in 1982 by the Constitution Act, which domesticated the Constitution of Canada by cutting the ties to the British constitution with the exception of the position of the Queen and her representatives in Canada.[9] Sections 91 and 92, the enumerations of legislative powers, were not affected to any great degree by the Constitution Act or a number of earlier amendments (in 1940, unemployment insurance had been added for the federation; in 1982, powers concerning non-renewable natural resources, forestry resources, and electrical energy were added for the provinces in Section 92A; an exemption for Quebec concerning education legislation was inserted in Section 93A in 1997, and old age pension powers were re-drafted for Section 94A in 1982, although they had already been created for the federation in 1951 and amended in 1964). This means that the formal distribution of legislative powers remains largely the same as in 1867, save for some later amendments and for adjustments that follow from interpretation by the supreme court instances of Canada (the Judicial Committee of the Privy Council until 1949, thereafter the Supreme Court) or from actual practice (see Sect. 4.2.1 and Chap. 5). Throughout the amendment procedure, Quebec was taken into account as a non-English territory of French provenance, featuring its own language and also its own legal and religious systems. During the period from the 1970s to the 1990s, the Canadian federation was involved in attempts to work out a new constitution, and in this process, Quebec requested and also received recognition of its particular position, but neither of the two constitutional amendment processes succeeded in securing the required majorities. Therefore, the position of Quebec as a part of the Canadian federation has remained complicated and subject to demands of independence, as evidenced by two referendums, one in 1980 and another in 1995, in which the independence alternative was not carried.

The Constitution Act 1867/1982, that is, the federal constitution, also contains provisions for the provinces on the basis of which the provinces operate directly:

---

[8]See, e.g., Légaré 2008.

[9]The Canadian Charter of Rights and Freedoms was enacted in 1982 as a part of the Constitution.

although some provinces have adopted constitutions of their own, several others have not done so. For instance, the Province of Quebec has not adopted a constitution, but organises its functions on the basis of the federal constitution and a number of pieces of law that have been enacted by the provincial legislature of Quebec as ordinary legislation but that may nonetheless be identified as legislation of a constitutional nature in Quebec.[10] Due in part to the fact that a portion of the constitutional norms take the form of constitutional conventions, the formal constitution that can be read from the constitutional texts is in many ways superseded by constitutional practice of a customary law nature. This is true, for instance, as concerns the position of the Queen as the head of state and her representatives in Canada (the Governor General at the federal level and the Lieutenant Governors in each of the provinces) as well as in respect of executive power both at the federal and provincial level with reference to the concept of responsible government.[11] At the same time, the federal constitution contains some provisions that are particular for Quebec or for Quebec and a number of other provinces.

It should be noted already at this stage that the provisions introducing certain asymmetries in the constitutional relationship between the federal level and the provincial level do not actually deal with the distribution of legislative powers between the federation and an individual province. Hence in principle, the distribution of legislative powers between the federal level and the provinces is symmetrical within the Constitution, meaning that all provinces have the same powers, although mechanisms exist in the ordinary law of the federation that allow some

[10]Such laws are the Election Act, An Act respecting the National Assembly, the Quebec Charter of Rights and Freedoms, the Charter of the French Language, the Charter on the Exercise of the Fundamental Rights and Prerogatives of the People of Quebec, and the Executive Power Act. See also Brun et al. 2008, pp. 18–19.

[11]See, e.g., Funston and Meehan 2003, p. 35, who summarize some of the main conventions involved in responsible government as follows: "1. the Governor General only acts on the advice of the Privy Council; 2. this Privy Council is not the full Council described in s. 13 of the Constitution Act, 1867, but rather is a much smaller subset, the Cabinet; 3. the Cabinet is chosen by the Prime Minister, and the number of ministers in it is up to him/her; 4. the Prime Minister, although mentioned nowhere in the Constitution Act, 1867, is the head of government; 5. the Prime Minister and his/her Cabinet must have the support of a majority of members in the House of Commons; 6. the Prime Minister and his/her Cabinet must have seats in the House of Commons or Senate; 7. House of Commons support for Prime Ministers and Cabinets is rallied by means of political parties; and 8. a failure to command the support of a majority of members in the House of Commons results in the government stepping down and, usually, the calling of a general election." See also Hogg 2014, s. 9.1. Other conventions mentioned by Funston and Meehan 2003, p. 35f., in a non-exclusive list of examples relate to "1. the exercise of prerogative powers of the Crown; 2. the operation of Parliament and the legislatures generally, including political parties and, at the national level, the relationship between the elected House of Commons and the appointed Senate; 3. the operation of the federal and provincial cabinets, ministers and civil services and the relationships among them; 4. federalism generally, aside from the formal division of powers, including reservation and disallowance of federal and provincial Acts, and the role of the federally appointed Lieutenant Governors in provincial matters; 5. the role of judges and courts in the governmental process and the independence of judges and courts from interference by the executive and legislative branches; […]".

particular arrangements for various provinces, most notably Quebec. In Canada, the method of distribution of legislative powers between the federal level and the provincial level is akin to the distribution of legislative powers in some autonomies, such as the Faroe Islands in Denmark and the Åland Islands in Finland. However, in addition, the practical functioning of federalism in Canada has resulted in some asymmetrical features that distinguish some provinces, such as Quebec, from the other provinces. Also, in comparison with other federal arrangements, it has been pointed out that "the distribution of powers in the Constitution of Canada is much less favourable to the federal power than would be suggested merely by comparing the text with that of the American or Australian Constitutions" and that "the present federal-provincial financial arrangements give the Canadian provinces more financial autonomy than is enjoyed by the states of the United States or Australia".[12]

The Åland Islands is an area which was an administrative part of the eastern part of Sweden until the Nordic War of 1808–1809, when the Russian Empire occupied what is today known as Finland and created it as a special jurisdiction. Åland was an integral part of this Grand Duchy of Finland, which in turn was an autonomous part of the Russian Empire until the independence of Finland in 1917. At this juncture, the population of the Åland Islands started to present claims of secession and re-unification with Sweden, and these claims were positively received in Sweden, which resulted in a diplomatic conflict between Finland and Sweden. This led to the enactment in 1920 of the Self-Government Act of Åland with provisions that any amendment to the Act would have to be decided by the method prescribed for the amendment of the Constitution, thus involving a two-thirds qualified vote. Furthermore, a requirement was added that any amendment to the Self-Government Act would require the consent of the Legislative Assembly of the Åland Islands given by a qualified majority of two-thirds.

The territorial dispute was resolved in 1921 by the Council of the League of Nations so as to deny secession from Finland under the condition that Finland supplemented the Self-Government Act, or Autonomy Act as it was termed by the League of Nations, with certain guarantees concerning the Swedish nature of the Åland Islands. However, this Åland Islands Settlement did not affect the distribution of legislative powers between the Parliament of Finland and the Legislative Assembly of the Åland Islands, other than by confirming in para. 1 the Self-Government Act and its scheme of distribution of powers.[13] At that point, the League of Nations also refrained from organizing a referendum on the national affiliation of the Åland Islands. The Constitution of Finland of course applies within

[12]Hogg 2014, s. 5.3(e).

[13]See the decision of the Council of the League of Nations of 24 June 1921, as supplemented on 27 June 1921 by the more concrete guarantees for the Åland Islands. This Åland Islands Settlement of June 1921 should not be confused with the Åland Islands Convention, that is, the Convention on the Non-Fortification and Neutralization of the Åland Islands, done in October 1921. See Suksi 2011, pp. 149–152.

the area of the Åland Islands, but the Self-Government Act makes exceptions to a portion of the Constitution, without setting aside the entire Constitution.

The 1920 Self-Government Act of Åland contained provisions concerning the distribution of legislative powers which established enumerated powers for the Parliament of Finland and residual powers for the Legislative Assembly of the Åland Islands. The main problem with this original determination of the legislative competences was that the practical operation of paras. 12 and 13 in section 9(2) of the 1920 Self-Government Act introduced unforeseen limitations to the competence of the Åland Islands. According to para. 12, the competence of the Parliament of Finland included those issues that were regulated through international treaties. Today, such a provision would, in the highly internationalized normative environment, have seriously threatened the legislative competence of Åland and transferred competence to the Parliament of Finland. In para. 13, the Parliament of Finland was given legislative competence in such areas as had not been normatively regulated in an ordinary act by the time of the enactment of the 1920 Self-Government Act. This provision, too, would have affected modern activities and issues that have been invented or arisen in society after 1920, and as a consequence, the regulation of new activities and issues would automatically have been placed within the legislative competence of the Parliament of Finland.

In retrospect, it is possible to conclude that the legislative competence of the Åland Islands would have been severely circumscribed and exposed to a continuous leakage of competence in the direction of the Parliament of Finland if these provisions had remained in force. With the definition of the competence of Åland that existed between 1920 and 1951, the legislative competence of the Åland Islands would today have been much more limited, while the legislative competence of the Parliament of Finland in the territorial jurisdiction of the Åland Islands would have been much broader. It was therefore in the interests of the Åland Islands to develop another system of distribution of legislative powers, and proposals in that direction were made as early as 1946. The technique of enumeration of the legislative powers of both legislatures resolved problematic issues, but when the 1951 Self-Government Act was being drafted, it was also recognized that the transition to a new system involving an enumeration of the competences of both legislatures could lead to new disputes concerning the interpretation of the competence line. In the event, Section 11 of the 1951 Self-Government Act listed the substantive areas in which the legislative power in regard of the jurisdiction of Åland would rest with the Parliament of Finland, while Section 13 listed those substantive areas where the legislative power could be exercised by the Legislative Assembly of the Åland Islands.[14]

In order to remedy the complicated issues in the 1920 Act and to stop inroads by national law-making powers into the competence sphere of Åland, the 1951 Self-Government Act thus re-designed the distribution of competences so as to establish two enumerations, one for the Parliament of Finland and another for the

---

[14]Suksi 2005, p. 173 f.

Legislative Assembly of the Åland Islands. This method of distribution of legislative powers was continued in the current Self-Government Act of 1991, but with longer lists of enumerations on each side. As pointed out above, this enumeration of two spheres of competence is a method for the division of powers also adopted by the Canadian federation, where the powers of both the federation and the provinces are based on enumeration.[15] However, in comparison with Canada, the distribution of legislative powers in Finland between the Parliament and the Legislative Assembly of the Åland Islands has not only been amended as to its point of departure so as to switch from a single list of enumeration to two lists of enumerations, but the material contents of the two enumerations have also undergone changes over the past 70 years.

The 1991 Self-Government Act, at Section 29, provides an additional, shorter list of competences for the Parliament of Finland which can be transferred to the Legislative Assembly of Åland by an ordinary piece of law enacted by simple majority in Parliament, provided that the Legislative Assembly gives its consent to such an Act. This easier method of transfer of powers has, however, never been used. Currently, a drafting process is underway in a parliamentary committee with a view to enacting a new Self-Government Act by the centennial of Ålandic autonomy around 2020–2022.[16] This future law may result in a remodelling of the distribution of legislative competences so as to maintain a shorter and more flexible enumeration for the Parliament of Finland while making the legislative competences of the Legislative Assembly of Åland residual or keeping them enumerated while making transfer of legislative power possible. In the latter case, transfer could take place, for instance, by decision of the Legislative Assembly of the Åland Islands, subject to consent by the Parliament of Finland, whereby the Legislative Assembly could move competence from the enumeration of the Parliament to its own list of enumerated powers. It is, however, too early to say with any certainty how a new act would fashion the distribution of legislative powers. The constitutional framework for the Åland Islands consists of the Constitution of Finland and the Self-Government Act (the Constitution is in effect in force in the Åland Islands to the extent it is not exempted by provisions in the Self-Government Act) and the 1975 Act on the Right to Acquire Real Estate in the Åland Islands. In addition, the exercise of Ålandic legislative powers is regulated by means of the 2011 Ålandic Act on the Rules of Procedure of Legislative Assembly and the 1971 Ålandic Act on the Government of the Åland Islands, both enacted on the basis of the legislative competence of the Åland Islands as established in the Self-Government Act.

---

[15]There is, however, no evidence in the *travaux preparatoires* concerning the 1951 Self-Government Act that the Canadian model would have been considered in the context of the Åland Islands, when the system of double enumeration was created. See Regeringens proposition RP 100/1946 rd till Riksdagen angående självstyrelselag för Åland and Regeringens proposition RP 38/1948 rd till Riksdagen angående självstyrelselag för Åland. As concerns distribution of competence, the government proposal aimed at eliminating the many problems of interpretation caused by the formulations in the single enumeration of the powers of the Parliament of Finland.

[16]See Ålands självstyrelse i utveckling 2017.

Up and until the Second World War, the Faroe Islands was more or less a regular county in Denmark.[17] During the war, Denmark proper was occupied by German forces and the Faroe Islands by British forces. This effectively cut off legitimate Danish governance in the area of the Faroe Islands. After the war, in 1946, a very small majority of the Faroese population expressed, in a referendum that had already been planned locally during the 1930s,[18] its wish to become independent from Denmark (perhaps inspired by Icelandic independence from Denmark in 1918/1944). This means that secession was on the table in a manner comparable to the Åland Islands in 1917–1921. Denmark did not consent to independence, but the Parliament of Denmark enacted an Act of Home Rule in 1948 that gave law-making powers to the Legislative Assembly of the Faroe Islands.[19]

The distribution of legislative powers between the Faroe Islands and Denmark was, until 2005, in principle in line with what could be expected of a territorial autonomy: between 1948 and 2005, the Danish Parliament retained those legislative powers that had not been transferred to the Faroe Islands. Under Section 6 of the 1948 Home Rule Act the residual powers were held by the national parliament, while the Legislative Assembly of the Faroe Islands had enumerated powers. In particular the enumerated powers included those enumerated in List A of the schedule to the Act, but additional matters mentioned in List B of the schedule to the Act could be transferred after further negotiations between the Danish and the Faroese authorities (see Sect. 3.3). At the same time, it is possible to conclude from the Act that not only the competences of the Faroe Islands were enumerated, but also to some extent the competences of the Danish Parliament, although the Parliament was, on the basis of Section 6 of the Home Rule Act, in possession of those competences that had not been transferred to the Faroe Islands. In this respect, some similarities can already at this point be noted between the Danish arrangement, on the one hand, and the Finnish and the Canadian arrangements, on the other, in that the distribution of competences was to some extent based on two enumerations. However, in principle, the Danish Parliament held the residual powers and Faroese territorial autonomy displayed the characteristics of a regular autonomy arrangement.

The 2005 Takeover Act introduced a fundamental change in the arrangements concerning the distribution of legislative competence. The Act establishes a prohibition of transfer of competence from the Parliament of Denmark to the Legislative Assembly of the Faroe Islands concerning a small number of enumerated matters while making it possible for the Faroe Islands to exercise the other

---

[17]However, the case has also been made that the Faroe Islands was a country within the Danish realm just as Norway had been until 1814 and Iceland until 1944. See speech by Eidesgaard 2006.

[18]See Sølvará 2003, p. 164.

[19]Lov nr. 137 af 23. Marts 1948 om Færøernes Hjemmestyre. However, in the beginning, the general understanding was that the self-government of the Faroe Islands was to some extent comparable to municipal self-government. See Sølvará 2003, p. 168.

competences.[20] The 2005 Act lists a number of matters and fields of law that require negotiations before a transfer of competence is possible, while not imposing such a requirement for some other competences. In addition, the Faroe Islands have received, under a separate 2005 Act on the Faroese Treaty Powers, a certain competence under international law to conclude international treaties.[21] The Act presupposes that the substantive area of the treaty belongs to the legislative competence of the Faroe Islands and that Denmark as a State has not exercised its treaty competence in relation to the matter regulated by the treaty. In the final instance, however, Denmark is liable for international commitments taken on by the Faroe Islands. The constitutional framework of the Faroe Islands is thus constituted by the 1953 Constitution of Denmark, the 1948 Home Rule Act, the 2005 Takeover Act and the 2005 Act on Faroese Treaty Powers as well as the 1994 Faroese Act on the Government of the Faroe Islands, which is enacted on the basis of the Home Rule Act.[22]

The 2005 Takeover Act divides the legislative competences of Denmark proper into three categories of matters, namely non-transferable, transferable after negotiations between the governments of Denmark and the Faroe Islands, and transferable without negotiations. In spite of the existence of this broad possibility of transfer from Parliament to the Legislative Assembly, there still remain competences with the Parliament that could be transferred but have not yet been

[20]For a description of the steps in the negotiations between the Danish and Faroese governments leading up to the adoption of the 2005 Takeover Act, see *travaux preparatoires*, Forslag til Lov om de færøske myndigheders overtagelse af sager og sagsområder, fremsat den 11. maj 2005 af statsministeren (Anders Fogh Rasmussen), section 1 of general aim and background.

[21]Lov nr. 579 af 24. Juni 2005 om Færøernes landsstyres indgåelse af folkeretlige aftaler. See Circular Note of the Ministry of Foreign Affairs of Denmark, Department of International Law (JTF. File No. 8.U.107), issued in Copenhagen on 7 November 2005 to all heads of diplomatic missions accredited to the Kingdom of Denmark, where treaty powers of the Faroe Islands and Greenland, established in two acts, one for each of the entities, are brought to the attention on the basis of the constitutional position of the two entities within the Danish Realm. At the same time as reference is made to the fact that the two acts are "in conformity with the right of self-determination of the People of the Faroes and the People of Greenland under international law". In the note, the Government of Denmark actually recognizes that the population of the Faroe Islands is a people entitled to self-determination, although that entitlement is not spelled out in positive Danish law in the same way it is spelled out for Greenland.

[22]For a consideration of the relationship between the 1948 Home Rule Act and the 2005 Takeover Act, see Forslag til Lov om de færøske myndigheders overtagelse af sager og sagsområder, fremsat den 11. maj 2005 af statsministeren (Anders Fogh Rasmussen), section 5. For a consideration of the relationship between the mechanism of taking over Danish legislative to the Faroe Islands, on the one hand, and the Danish Constitution, on the other, see appendix 1 to the proposal (Bilag 1: Notat om grænserne for overladelse af sager og sagsområder til de færøske myndigheder af hensyn til rigsenheden og særlige bestemmelser i grundloven), where section 3.2. concludes that the Constitution of Denmark applies in all parts of the Danish Realm and where section 3.5. concludes that it is a firm presumption that the legislative power can transfer (delegate) its competence, albeit under restrictions that follow from Section 3(1) of the Danish Constitution.

transferred. The system for the distribution of legislative competence in the 2005 Takeover Act creates a procedure by which the law-maker of the Faroe Islands transfers competences from the Parliament of Denmark by means of its own transfer decisions, clad in the form of formal Faroese legislation. Apart from establishing a dynamic system that contrasts with the formal distribution of legislative powers under the Canadian Constitution and also under current the Finnish Act on the Self-Government of the Åland Islands, this leads to a situation where different elements of Faroese competence are established in a number of different legislative enactments of the Legislative Assembly of the Faroe Islands enacted at different points of time, producing a fragmentary legislative situation of which it is not easy to gain an overview.

It appears that in addition to the duality expressed in the distribution of legislative powers, the three states are also good examples for the purposes of this comparison for reasons related to the regional identities that the states have been trying to address. In two of the states, Denmark and Finland, the quest for another identity resulted in attempts of secession and, as a consequence, grants of autonomy, while in Canada, the quest for separate identity resulted in such attempts in Quebec only a good century after the distribution of legislative power had been instituted. Therefore, although the historical background does not necessarily give the comparison between the three situations a perfect platform beyond the method of distribution of legislative powers, the similarities are close enough to be of some value. In addition, the fundamental norms upon which the three examples of distribution of legislative powers are based display somewhat differing constitutional status: whilst the distribution of powers is included in the formal constitution in Canada, the two enumerations are part of an act considered in Finland to be of a constitutional nature, and in Denmark, the legislation on the distribution of legislative powers is formally speaking ordinary law, although it has been enacted on the basis of an agreement between the two governments. Therefore, the caveat must be issued that the interpretative strategies employed by the bodies entrusted with competence adjudication and with resolution of concrete cases with a competence dimension may differ because of the formal position of the fundamental legislation.[23] However, the impact of the formal basis of the fundamental act in the hierarchy of norms is likely to be lesser than the impact of the fact that the double enumerations analysed here are products of three different legal orders.

[23]See Craig and Walters 2000, pp. 229–233, where the authors distinguish between statutory interpretation and constitutional interpretation and indicate that they are essentially different in nature. While this may be so in the Commonwealth context and against the background of the praxis of the Privy Council, the relevance of the distinction for other, very different jurisdictions is likely to be very limited.

References

Ålands självstyrelse i utveckling (2017) Ålandskommitténs 2013 slutbetänkande. Justitieministeriets publikation—betänkanden och utlåtanden 33/2017. Justitieministeriet, Helsingfors
Brun H, Tremblay G, Brouillet E (2008) Droit constitutionnel, 5e edn. Les Éditions Yvon Blais Inc., Cowansville (Quebec)
Craig P, Walters M (2000) The courts, devolution and judicial review. In: Forsyth C (ed) Judicial review and the constitution. Hart Publishing, Oxford and Portland, Oregon, pp 213–244
Eidesgaard J (2006) 'Færøernes forfatningsmæssige stilling', speech at Nordic Lawyers' Academy on 24 August 2006 in Tórshavn, the Faroe Islands (on file with author)
Forslag til Lov om de færøske myndigheders overtagelse af sager og sagsområder, fremsat den 11. maj 2005 af statsministeren
Funston BW, Meehan ER (2003) Canada's constitutional law in a Nutshell, 3rd edn. Thomson Professional Pub Canada, Toronto
Hogg PW (2014) Constitutional law of Canada, 5th ed supplemented, vols 1 and 2. Thomson & Carswell, Toronto
Inwood GJ (2013) Understanding Canadian federalism—an introduction to theory and practice. Pearson, Toronto
Légaré A (2008) 'Canada's experiment with Aboriginal self-determination in Nunavut: from vision to illusion. Int J Minor Group Rights 15:335
Regeringens Proposition RP 100/1946 rd till Riksdagen angående självstyrelselag för Åland
Regeringens Proposition RP 38/1948 rd till Riksdagen angående självstyrelselag för Åland
Smith DE (2010) Federalism and the constitution of Canada. University of Toronto Press, Toronto
Sølvará HA (2003) Færøernes statsretlige stilling i historisk belysning – mellem selvstyre og selvbestemmelse. Faroese Law Rev 3:145
Suksi M (2011) Sub-state governance through territorial autonomy. Springer, Heidelberg
Suksi M (2005) Ålands konstitution. Åbo Akademis förlag, Åbo

Chapter 3
Material Content of Enumerations

3.1 Canada and the Provinces: A Mix of Law-Making Powers for Both Orders of Government

In the continental European legal tradition, a division of the legal order into public law and private law is carried out on grounds which generally imply that legislation which establishes a vertical relationship of a non-dispositive nature between public authorities and individuals, including public powers for authorities to make decisions concerning individuals on the basis of provisions in legislation, is a matter of public law, whereas legislation which creates the platform for a horizontal relationship of a dispositive nature between individuals or enterprises is a matter of private law. Criminal law and law of procedure are normally included in public law. A similar distinction between public law and private law is observed in common law countries such as Canada, where, for example, constitutional, administrative, criminal, and other areas of regulatory law (such as environmental law and tax law) are understood as areas of public law, while areas such as tort law, contract law and property law are considered areas of private law.[1]

Sections 91 and 92 of the Canadian Constitution do not seem to follow any theoretical model for the distribution of legislative powers (or division of powers, which is the term often used in Canadian legal language),[2] but result instead from a practical grouping of matters. The federation is in charge of those powers, which are outside the portion of common law which was the domain of the various parts of the British territories in North America before 1867, and outside the portion of the

[1]Craik et al. 2011, p. 1. For a British view into public law, see Barnett 2010, p. 1, and Le Sueur et al. 2010, pp. 3–9. Without doubt, the distinction between public law and private law is in many ways problematic, and in a modern society, they are also increasingly mixing with each other.

[2]For the lists of powers in the Canadian Constitution, Sections 91–95, see http://laws-lois.justice.gc.ca/eng/Const//page-4.html#docCont (accessed on 4 January 2018). For an analysis of the material contents of legislative powers in Sections 91 and 92, see Hogg 2014, from s. 18.1 until s. 33.5. See also Inwood 2013, p. 9.

M. Suksi, *Double Enumeration of Legislative Powers in a Sub-State Context*, SpringerBriefs in Law, https://doi.org/10.1007/978-3-319-90921-9_3

civil law that was traditionally practiced in the French-speaking parts of the territory.[3] The solution was doubtless very pragmatic at that juncture. However, with the development of society, the double list has been exposed to challenges that have required some (albeit relatively limited) amendments and, of course, interpretation of where the competence lies, in particular when new legislative matters have emerged as a result of social, economic or technological development (see below, Chap. 5). The distribution of legislative powers is also complicated by the fact that according to Section 132, the federation is in possession of treaty powers and powers relating to foreign affairs.

The various areas of legislation and legislative matters are fashioned in the legal language of the 19th century, but an attempt can nonetheless be made to fit them into the categories of public law and private law, albeit admittedly in a crude fashion. In some instances, the matter as identified in the Canadian Constitution may fall into two parts, one belonging to public law (such as navigation in para. 10 of Section 91) and the other to private law (such as shipping in para. 10 of Section 91).

Federal matters falling into the sphere of public law would, by and large, include the following, listed in the order they appear in Section 91, complemented with one federal head of power from Section 92:

> Public debt and property; unemployment insurance; the raising of money by any mode or system of taxation; the borrowing of money on public credit; the postal service; the census and statistics; militia, military and naval services, and defence; the fixing of and providing for the salaries and allowances of civil servants and other officers of the government of Canada; beacons, buoys, lighthouses, and Sable Island; navigation; quarantine and the establishment and maintenance of marine hospitals; currency and coinage; the issue of paper money; patents of invention and discovery; legal tender; Indians, and lands reserved for the Indians; naturalization and aliens; criminal law, except the constitution of courts of criminal jurisdiction, but including procedure in criminal matters; the establishment, maintenance, and management of penitentiaries, local works and undertakings [assigned to the federation in Section 92, para. 10 –MS] concerning (a) lines of steam or other ships, railways, canals, telegraphs, and other works and undertakings connecting the province with any other or others of the provinces, or extending beyond the limits of the province, (b) lines of steam ships between the province and any British or foreign country, and (c) such works as, although wholly situate within the province, are before or after their execution declared by the Parliament of Canada to be for the general advantage of Canada or for the advantage of two or more of the provinces.

In addition, under Section 94A, the Parliament of Canada may make laws in relation to old age pensions and supplementary benefits, including survivors' and disability benefits irrespective of age. However, here there is an interesting inverted supremacy clause in operation, because no such law shall affect the operation of any law present or future of a provincial legislature in relation to any such matter. Therefore, a provincial law-maker may pass legislation that derogates from federal law in this area and sets aside federal law. This is a unique feature of Canadian

---

[3]See Hogg 2014, s. 5.1(g) for a comment from the point of view of subsidiarity.

federalism in comparison with other federations and turns the classical federal preemption constellations upside down.

Federal matters falling into the sphere of private law would, by and large, contain the following, listed in the order they appear in Section 91:

> The regulation of trade and commerce; shipping; sea coast and inland fisheries; ferries between a province and any British or foreign country or between two provinces; banking; incorporation of banks; savings banks; weights and measures; bills of exchange and promissory notes; interest; bankruptcy and insolvency; copyrights; and marriage and divorce.

No doubt, persons coming from different legal backgrounds could classify these matters slightly differently according to their public law or private law nature. However, the classification indicates that the federation is, by and large, in charge of legislating about some core functions of law and order within the area of public law, while leaving important material areas of public law to the provinces (see below).[4] At the same time, the federation is in charge of some fundamental areas of legislation in the sphere of private law, while an important part of that competence, namely property and civil rights in the province, is legislative competence of the provinces.

Provincial matters falling into the sphere of public law would, by and large, contain the following on the basis of Section 92:

> Direct taxation within the province in order to raise revenue for provincial purposes; the borrowing of money on the sole credit of the province; the establishment and tenure of provincial offices and the appointment and payment of provincial officers; the management and sale of public lands belonging to the province and of the timber and wood thereon; the establishment, maintenance and management of public and reformatory prisons in and for the province; the establishment, maintenance and management of hospitals, asylums, charities, and eleemosynary institutions in and for the province, other than marine hospitals; municipal institutions in the province; shop, saloon, tavern, auctioneer, and other licences to raise revenue for provincial, local, or municipal purposes; local works and undertakings other than such as are of the […] classes [assigned to the federation –MS][5]; the administration of justice in the province, including the constitution, maintenance and organization of provincial courts, both of civil and of criminal jurisdiction, and including procedure in civil matters in those courts; the imposition of punishment by fine, penalty, or

[4]As pointed out in Leclair 2010, p. 567: "Parliament's enumerated powers are, for the most part, 'electorally unattractive'. Interprovincial transportation, communications and national defence might have had some appeal in 1867, but with the advent of the welfare state, health, social welfare and education have become the politicians' preferred fields of battle. The sorrowful nature—if I may be allowed this expression—of the central government's enumerated heads of power explains the enthusiastic recourse to the spending power witnessed during the 1960s through the 1980s and beyond. However, in view of the spending power's dubious constitutionality in the eyes of many, the central government has tried, quite legitimately, to find ways of expanding its existing legislative powers."

[5]As pointed out in Hogg 2014, s. 5.3(i), "[t]he federal Parliament's power under s. 92(10)(c) to bring a local work within federal jurisdiction by declaring it to be 'for the general advantage of Canada' was frequently used in the past, mainly in respect of local railways. It has been used only sparingly in recent years."

> imprisonment for enforcing any law of the province made in relation to any matter coming within any of the classes of subjects enumerated in this Section; generally all matters of a merely local [or private –see below; MS] nature in the province.

Matters listed in Section 92A concerning non-renewable natural resources, forestry resources and electrical energy also belong to the public law sphere of the province: exploration for non-renewable natural resources in the province; development, conservation and management of non-renewable natural resources and forestry resources in the province, including laws in relation to the rate of primary production therefrom; development, conservation and management of sites and facilities in the province for the generation and production of electrical energy; laws in relation to the raising of money by any mode or system of taxation of a non-discriminatory nature concerning production exported to another part of Canada and production not exported from the province in respect of (a) non-renewable natural resources and forestry resources in the province and the primary production therefrom, and (b) sites and facilities in the province for the generation of electrical energy and the production therefrom. Finally, education, a matter listed in Section 93, belongs to the provinces within the sphere of public law, with some exceptions concerning denominational schools and educational establishments created during the pre-federation time, where the federation has powers (except, according to Section 93A, in Quebec, where the province has more powers in relation to such special schools).[6]

In Section 92A, however, there exists an explicit concurrent jurisdiction between the federation and the provinces. According to para. 2 of the Section, "in each province, the legislature may make laws in relation to the export from the province to another part of Canada of the primary production from non-renewable natural resources and forestry resources in the province and the production from facilities in the province for the generation of electrical energy, but such laws may not authorize or provide for discrimination in prices or in supplies exported to another part of Canada". Para. 3 of the same section continues by stating that "nothing in subsection (2) derogates from the authority of Parliament to enact laws in relation to the matters referred to in that subsection and, where such a law of Parliament and a law of a province conflict, the law of Parliament prevails to the extent of the conflict". Within this relatively narrow material area of concurrent powers, there is thus a supremacy clause in operation that gives preeminence to federal legislation in situations of conflict. In para. 6 of the Section, there is a limitation of derogation with respect to powers enjoyed by the provinces on the basis of their own legislative competences prior to the entering into force of the constitutional provision in 1982. Further, within the sphere of public law, concerning the provinces of Ontario, Nova Scotia, and New Brunswick, the Parliament of Canada has the unrestricted power, under Section 94, to make provision for the uniformity of all or any of the laws

[6]As pointed out in Hogg 2014, s.5.3(h), the federal power under Section 93 to "enact remedial laws to correct provincial incursions on minority educational rights has never been exercised, and has in practice become 'obsolete'".

relative to procedural law of all or any of the courts in those three states. However, such uniformity law shall not have any effect in any province unless the provincial legislature, too, enacts this as law. Such doubling of the law-making procedure for the entering into force of an ordinary act appears to be a stricter requirement than the requirement of consent in the context of the Åland Islands and, in fact, establishes a provincial veto.

Moreover, according to Section 95, agriculture in the province and immigration into the province is, in principle and originally, a legislative competence of the province. However, the Parliament of Canada is also empowered to make laws in relation to agriculture in all or any of the provinces, and immigration into all or any of the provinces, which means that with respect to these matters, there is a completely concurrent jurisdiction. Therefore, the provision creates a preemption principle by stating that for such federal legislation concerning agriculture and immigration, any provincial law on the same matter shall have effect in and for the province as long and as far only as it is not contradictory to any Act of the Parliament of Canada.

Provincial matters falling into the sphere of private law would, by and large, containing the following on the basis of Section 92:

> The incorporation of companies with provincial objects; the solemnization of marriage in the province; property and civil rights in the province; generally all matters of a merely [local or –see above; MS] private nature in the province.

Notably, the category of 'property and civil rights in the province' is a very broad one and gives the provincial legislature a large private-law area within which to legislate. However, concerning the provinces of Ontario, Nova Scotia, and New Brunswick, the Parliament of Canada has the unrestricted power, under Section 94, to make provision for the uniformity of all or any of the laws relating to property and civil rights. However, such uniformity law shall not have any effect in any province unless the provincial legislature, too, enacts this as law. As pointed out above, such doubling of the law-making procedure appears to be a stricter requirement than the requirement of consent in the context of the Åland Islands.

Again, persons coming from different legal backgrounds could classify these matters slightly differently according to the public law or private law nature of the matter. However, this classification indicates that the provinces are, by and large, in charge of legislating in many important substantive fields of law within the sphere of public law, such as education, social affairs (as local matters), health, and environment. At the same time, the provinces are in charge of a number of fundamental legislative matters in the sphere of private law, most notably property and civil rights in the province. By and large, it seems on the basis of the two enumerations as if the provinces are in possession of more legislative powers than the federal law-maker. From a material point of view, for the enactment of laws of general application, it appears as if the provincial legislatures were more important law-makers in Canada for private individuals and business enterprises than the federation. Actual practice may, however, contradict this conclusion (see Sect. 4.2.1). Both levels, notably, have powers of taxation.

3.2 Finland and the Åland Islands: Competence Mainly in Public Law

Within the matters mentioned in Section 27 of the 1991 Self-Government Act, the legislative powers of the Finnish Parliament apply to the Åland Islands in addition to mainland Finland, while the Legislative Assembly of the Åland Islands is, at the same time, empowered to enact legislation on matters listed in Section 18 of the Act for application in the Åland Islands.[7] As can be seen from the enumeration of the powers of the Parliament of Finland for the purposes of the jurisdiction of Åland, they are to a great extent focused on rules that in the continental European doctrine are placed in the sphere of private law. This is reinforced under para. 41, according to which private law matters not mentioned in section 27 belong to the legislative competence of the Parliament of Finland, unless the matter relates directly to an area of legislation within which the competence is with the Legislative Assembly.

The presumption therefore in the jurisdiction of Åland is that private law is mainly for the Parliament of Finland, while public law remains to a great extent a responsibility of the Legislative Assembly of the Åland Islands. In addition, the presumption of competence for the Parliament of Finland is promoted in the area of criminal law and the deprivation of individual liberty by the fact that the general power of criminalization in respect of the criminal code is allocated under Section 27, para. 22, to the Parliament of Finland, while the Legislative Assembly is empowered under Section 18, para. 25 to criminalize conduct which falls within the legislative competence of the Åland Islands. As is evident on the basis of Section 27, para. 23, the competence to regulate courts and the administration of justice is vested in the state, and therefore state courts exercise jurisdiction on the Åland Islands. Hence the administration of justice is provided for under legislation enacted by the Parliament of Finland. However, the state courts try cases not only on the basis of acts of the Parliament of Finland, but also on the basis of acts of the Legislative Assembly. This has functioned well, because the courts are, naturally, independent in relation to both the Åland Islands and the state of Finland. Treaty powers are exercised by the government and Parliament of Finland, but in order for a treaty that touches upon the legislative competence of Åland to enter into force within the jurisdiction of the Åland Islands, the Legislative Assembly has to give its consent to such a treaty by means of a resolution, which is not a legislative enactment.

Under Sections 27 and 29 of the Self-Government Act, the following issues of a public law nature are under the legislative competence of the Parliament of Finland in respect of the Åland Islands:

---

[7]For the two enumerations, see the English translation of the 1991 Self-Government Act, as amended by 2011, at http://www.lagtinget.ax/text.con?iPage=59&m=228 (accessed on 4 January 2018).

The enactment, amendment or repeal of the Constitution and an exception to the Constitution; the right to reside in the country, to choose a place of residence and to move from one place to another; the exercise of freedom of speech, freedom of association and freedom of assembly; confidentiality of post and telecommunications; the organization and activities of state officials; foreign relations, subject to the provisions of chapters 9 and 9 a; the flag and coat of arms of the state and the use thereof, with the exceptions provided by section 18, para. 3; patents; merchant shipping and shipping lanes; aviation; the pricing of agricultural and fishing industry products and the promotion of the export of agricultural products; the formation and registration of pieces of real property and connected duties; mineral finds and mining, with the exceptions as provided by section 18, para. 19; nuclear energy (however, the consent of the Government of Åland is required for the construction, possession and operation of a nuclear power plant and the handling and stockpiling of materials therefor in Åland); criminal law, with the exceptions provided by section 18, para. 25; judicial proceedings, subject to the provisions of sections 25 and 26; preliminary investigations, the enforcement of convictions and sentences and the extradition of offenders; the administrative deprivation of personal liberty; the Church Code and other legislation relating to religious communities and the right to hold a public office regardless of creed; citizenship, legislation on aliens, passports; firearms and ammunition; civil defense (however, the decision to evacuate residents of Åland to a place outside Åland may only be made with the consent of the Government of Åland); human contagious diseases, castration and sterilization, abortion, artificial insemination and forensic medical investigations; the qualifications of persons involved in health care and nursing; the pharmacy service, medicines and pharmaceutical products, drugs and the production of poisons and the determination of the uses thereof; contagious diseases in pets and livestock; the prohibition of the import of animals and animal products; the prevention of substances destructive to plants from entering the country; the armed forces and border guards (subject to the provisions of section 12), the actions of the authorities to ensure the security of the state, state of defense and readiness for a state of emergency; explosive substances, to the extent relating to state security; taxes and dues, with the exceptions provided by section 18, para. 5; the issuance of paper money, foreign currencies; statistics necessary for the state; archive material derived from state officials, subject to the provisions of section 30, para. 17; telecommunications (however, a state official may only grant permission to engage in general telecommunications in Åland with the consent of the Government of Åland); population registers; the trade register, the association register and the shipping register; employment pensions of employees and elected officials of the municipalities, and employment pensions of other persons, with the exceptions provided by section 18, subparagraph 2a, as well as other social insurance; alcohol legislation other than that referred to in section 18, subparagraph 13.

The following legislative powers of the Parliament of Finland in relation to the territory of Åland appear to be of a more private law nature:

Surname and forename, guardianship, the declaration of the legal death of a person; marriage and family relations, the juridical status of children, adoption and inheritance with the exceptions provided by section 10; associations and foundations, companies and other private corporations and the keeping of accounts; the general nationwide preconditions on the right of foreigners and foreign corporations to own and possess real property and shares of stock and to practice a trade; copyright, design copyright and trademarks; unfair business practices, promotion of competition and consumer protection; insurance contracts; foreign trade; units, gauges and methods of measurement, standardization; the production and stamping of precious metals and trade in items containing precious metals; labour law, with the exception of collective agreements on the salaries of Åland and municipal officials, and subject to the provisions of section 29, paragraph 1, para. 6, and section 29, para. 2; other matters under private law not specifically mentioned in this section, unless the matters relate

> directly to an area of legislation within the competence of Åland according to this Act; other matters that are deemed to be within the legislative power of the Parliament of Finland according to the principles underlying this Act; banking and credit services; employment contracts, with the exception provided for apprenticeship by section 18, subparagraph 14, and co-operation in enterprises.

According to Section 17 of the Self-Government Act, the Legislative Assembly of the Åland Islands shall enact legislation for Åland, and the actual legislative powers of the Legislative Assembly are listed in Section 18 of the Act. The list of legislative powers of the Åland Islands comprises a total of 27 paragraphs. As established in Section 18, Åland shall have legislative powers in the territory of Åland in respect of the following issues of a public law nature:

> The organization and duties of the Legislative Assembly of the Åland Islands and the election of its members, the Government of Åland and the officials and services subordinate to it; the officials of Åland, collective agreements on salaries of the employees of Åland and the disciplinary punishment of Åland officials; employment pensions of the employees of Åland and the elected representatives in the administration of Åland, as well as of head teachers, teachers and temporary teachers in primary and lower secondary schools in Åland; the flag and coat of arms of Åland and the use thereof in Åland, the use of the Åland flag on vessels of Åland and on merchant vessels, fishing vessels, pleasure boats and other comparable vessels whose home port is in Åland, without limiting the right of state offices and services or of private persons to use the flag of the state; municipal boundaries, municipal elections, municipal administration and the officials of municipalities, collective agreements on the salaries of municipal officials and the disciplinary punishment of municipal officials; additional tax on income for Åland and provisional extra income tax, as well as trade and amusement taxes, the bases of dues levied for Åland and municipal tax; public order and security, with the exceptions provided by section 27, paras. 27, 34 and 35; the firefighting and rescue service; building and planning, adjoining properties, housing; the appropriation of real property and of special rights required for public use in exchange for full compensation, with exceptions provided by section 61; the protection of nature and the environment, the recreational use of nature, water law; prehistoric relics and the protection of buildings and artifacts with cultural and historical value; health care and medical treatment, with the exceptions provided by section 27, paras. 24, 29 and 30; burial by cremation; social welfare; licenses to serve alcoholic beverages; education, apprenticeship, culture, sport and youth work; the archive, library and museum service, with the exceptions provided by section 27, para. 39; farming and forestry, the regulation of agricultural production (provided that the state officials concerned are consulted prior to the enactment of legislation on the regulation of agricultural production); hunting and fishing, the registration of fishing vessels and the regulation of the fishing industry; prevention of cruelty to animals and veterinary care, with exceptions as provided by section 27, paras. 31, 33; the maintenance of the productive capacity of farmlands, forests and fishing waters; the duty to transfer, in exchange for full compensation, unutilized or partially utilized farmland or fishing water into the possession of another person to be used for these purposes, for a fixed period; the right to prospect for, lay claim to and utilize mineral finds; the postal service and the right to broadcast by radio or cable in Åland, with the limitations consequential on section 27, para. 4; roads and canals, road traffic, railway traffic, boat traffic, local shipping lanes; promotion of employment; statistics on conditions in Åland; the creation of a criminal offence and the extent of the penalty for such an offence in respect of a matter falling within the legislative competence of Åland; the imposition of a threat of a fine and the implementation thereof, as well as the use of other means of coercion in respect of a matter falling within the legislative competence of Åland; other matters deemed to be within the legislative power of Åland in accordance with the principles underlying this Act.

It is important to understand that the Self-Government Act, aside from mentioning the governmental institutions at the sub-state level, leaves these institutions and organs to be regulated by enactments of the Legislative Assembly. The Act specifies in Section 3(2) that the administration of Åland is vested in the Government of Åland and the officials subordinate to it. It further stipulates in Section 3(1) that the population of the Åland Islands is, in matters relating to autonomy, represented by the Legislative Assembly. The members of this Legislative Assembly shall, according to Section 13, be elected by direct and secret ballot, through universal and equal suffrage. Because only persons with the right of domicile shall be entitled under Section 9 to participate in these elections, universal suffrage in elections to the Legislative Assembly is implemented within that group of persons. Thus the internal structures of government or the actual "material constitution" of the Åland Islands is determined by Ålandic legislation, so much so that the Legislative Assembly can also decide to place a requirement of a two-thirds majority for the amendment of pieces of law that it considers more important than regular pieces of law.[8] However, the scope of the internal authority of the Legislative Assembly to pass legislation on these issues, either by simple majority or qualified majority is established by Section 18.

According to Section 18, Åland shall have legislative powers in the territory of Åland in respect of the following issues of a private law nature:

> Tenancy and rent regulation, lease of land; trade, subject to the provisions of Section 11, Section 27, paras. 2, 4, 9, 12–15, 17–19, 26, 27, 29–34, 37 and 40, and Section 29, paragraph 1, paras. 3–5, with the exception that the Legislative Assembly of Åland also has the power to impose measures to foster trade referred to in the said paragraphs.

Because most of the Ålandic powers are in the sphere of public law, they clearly imply the need for and existence of relatively broad administrative decision-making machinery for implementation of the Acts of Åland in individual cases. In fact, the public sector of the Åland Islands appears, proportionally speaking, to be greater than that of mainland Finland, partly because of this clear public law orientation and partly because of the independent Ålandic control over transfer of the equalisation amount from the state budget to the Åland Islands. Due to the improved performance of the Ålandic economy and the consequent increase in the tax revenue that the state collected in the Åland Islands, these equalisation amounts saw a steady increase during the 1990s, resulting in a corresponding enlargement of the public administration of the Åland Islands.

In comparison with Canada and also the Faroe Islands (see Sect. 3.3), the position of private law is remarkably limited within the legislative powers of the Åland Islands. On the other hand, because private law is currently much more international and "common" to different countries than the more nationally or locally oriented public law, the range of what a sub-state entity could do within

[8]This power of creating an internal constitutional distinction between ordinary legislation enacted by simple majority and particular legislation enacted by the qualified majority of two-thirds has not been used but occasionally. See Suksi 2011, pp. 157–158.

private law is in practice very limited, unless it aims at creating, for instance, direct or indirect trade barriers that have an impact on economic activities.

3.3 Denmark and the Faroe Islands: Sub-state Entity in Charge of Its Own Competence

The legislative powers of the Danish Parliament with regard to the Faroe Islands are, at least in principle, rather limited. Under Section 1(2) of the 2005 Takeover Act, it is established that five matters are not transferable to the Faroe Islands. These matters, which all belong to the sphere of public law, thus constitute the core of the legislative powers of the Danish Parliament in the territory of the Faroe Islands:[9]

> The Constitution; citizenship; the Supreme Court; foreign-, security- and defence policy; and currency and fiscal policy.

In the sphere of private law, no limits for transferring legislative powers exist. Therefore, in principle, the national enumeration could be empty as concerns private law.

Conversely, the legislative powers of the Legislative Assembly of the Faroe Islands appear to be very extensive in the sphere of public law; in fact, almost complete with respect to the public powers that affect an individual in her or his dealings with government, or in terms of criminal law. This is, in principle, even clearer within the sphere of private law, where the Legislative Assembly could have complete powers over all norms of a horizontal nature. However, the fact that the 2005 Takeover Act exists does not mean that all of those powers that can be transferred actually have been transferred from the Parliament to the Legislative Assembly by the decisions of the latter.

As was explained above, the current normative framework for the distribution of legislative powers is constituted by two Acts of the Danish Parliament, the first being the 1948 Home Rule Act, in which there are two lists of powers or schedules listing powers, the so-called List A and List B. Most of the matters on List A were transferred to the Faroe Islands immediately in 1948 or soon thereafter, whilst some of the powers have been exercised by the Parliament through national framework legislation applicable to the entire country on the basis of Section 9 of the 1948

[9] For an explanation of what these matters entail in terms of substantive law, see Forslag til Lov om de færøske myndigheders overtagelse af sager og sagsområder, fremsat den 11. maj 2005 af statsministeren (Anders Fogh Rasmussen), section 4. As pointed out in section 6.3., the Faroese authorities would also not have competence to determine, which general rules there exist for the activities that Danish authorities exercise in the Faroe Islands, such as particular duties of staff persons with Danish authorities, and that civil service legislation for Danish authorities in the Faroe Islands will continue to be a competence of the Parliament of Denmark.

Home Rule Act. List B contains matters which could be transferred from the Parliament to the Faroe Islands after negotiations between the Danish and Faroese governments. It seems that between 1948 and 2005, praxis on what could be transferred to the competence of the Faroe Islands was initially relatively restrictive, but became more permissive over the years so as to encompass, on the basis of negotiations, matters that were not explicitly mentioned in List B. Finally, in 2002, a common declaration between the leaders of the government of Denmark and the Faroe Islands expressed the idea of further cooperation on transfer to the Faroe Islands of more legislative matters within the framework of the Constitution and the Danish Commonwealth.[10] A portion of the legislative powers mentioned on both List A and List B are still with the Parliament of Denmark and have not been transferred to the Legislative Assembly of the Faroe Islands either on the basis of the 1948 Home Rule Act or the 2005 Takeover Act, at least not yet (see below).[11]

The greater part of matters and fields of law on the so-called List A of the 1948 Act was placed with the Faroe Islands straight away in 1948, or thereafter at the request of the Legislative Assembly or the national government. List A contained the following fields (including also more specific matters):

(1) Local Faroese administration within the framework of the new system (including within this framework rules governing the Legislative Assembly, elections to the Legislative Assembly, administrative regulations, initiation, adoption, approval and publication of legislation enacted by the Legislative Assembly, appointment, dismissal, conditions of service, salaries and pensions of Faroese civil servants);
(2) municipal affairs (including local government administration, supervision and taxation);
(3) building, fire service, town planning, housing, rent, population register;
(4) health services, medical practise, midwifery, hospital service, apothecaries (including: public medical officers, legislation on unqualified practising of medical profession, eradication of tuberculosis and other contagious diseases, care of mental patients, vaccination);
(5) public welfare services, public assistance, national insurance, compulsory accident insurance, labour, apprentices, assistants, holidays;
(6) direct and indirect taxes (including stamp duties, totalised duties, duties on special Faroese lottery. while handling charges such as legal fees and land registration fees shall accrue to the authority which defrays the cost of the institution concerned);
(7) licensing and, in general, disposal of own income and expenditure, accounting regulations, audits and appropriation of own receipts and expenditures;
(8) approval of harbour duties;
(9) schools (including elementary schools, secondary schools and courses, teachers' training, people's high schools, post-primary schools and vocational schools, such as commercial schools, technical schools, navigation schools, etc.);
(10) archives, libraries, museums (except national archives; reservation is made for compulsory deliveries to the Royal Library);
(11) protected buildings, nature conservancy;

[10]Rasmussen 2002, pp. 377–380.

[11]For English-language versions of the 1948 Home Rule Act and the 2005 Takeover Act, see http://stm.dk/_p_13089.html (accessed on 4 January 2018).

(12) harbours, coastal protection, canals, hydraulic plant, traffic (including roads, railways, tramways, ferry services, bus services and road haulage), motor and traffic, local post, telegraph and telephone services, electrical installations;
(13) rural and agricultural matters (including general rural legislation, copyhold tenure, tenancy, parcelling of land, exchanges of strip-holdings, smallholdings, plant cultivation, animal husbandry, horticulture, agriculture related occupations, soil improvement, forestry), veterinary services, pest control, domestic animals, arbitration, protection of animals, legislation on dogs, territorial hunting and protection of animals, territorial fishing and protection of fish, land registration;
(14) licensing of theatres and cinemas, entertainment, collections and lotteries, shipwrecks, property lost and found, toxic substances, explosives, arms;
(15) supplies, production and distribution, price control, price ceilings, rationing, discounts and subsidies, restrictions on bonuses and dividends, peddling of goods, rules governing alcoholic beverages, shop closing rules, catering, trade licensing, trade and association registers, registers of ships, brokers, state-authorized translators, average adjusters, state-authorized measurers and weighers, auditors, storage facilities, commission, agents, commercial travellers, agents of foreign firms, book-keeping, mortgage credit institutes, etc., local insurance activities;
(16) local public trustees, cadastral system, tourism, expropriation of land for specific uses, provisions governing the production of printed matters, provisions concerning special time rules, civic duties, equal rights for men and women.

Some of these List A competences were (and still are) exercised within framework legislation established by the Danish Parliament for the entire state and which were viewed as matters common to the Realm.[12] The so-called List B of the 1948 Act on Home Rule contained matters which could be transferred to the Faroe Islands after negotiations between the governments of Denmark and the Faroe Islands. List B contained the following fields (including also more specific matters):

(1) The Established Church (including all aspects of church organisation, rituals, church officials, their salaries and pensions, church buildings, churchyards, admission into and withdrawal from the Established Church, congregations formed by voluntary association of parishioners, release of parishioners from the obligation to use the services of the incumbent clergyman, dissenting creeds, public holidays legislation);
(2) police;
(3) underground deposits of raw materials, radio, aviation;
(4) the land fund;
(5) import and export controls.

[12]See Oversigt over sagsområder overtaget af de færøske myndigheder, at http://www.stm.dk/multimedia/FO_DK_oversigt_sagsomraader_010811.pdf (accessed on 2 February 2018), which indicates that of matters in List A, everything has been taken over by the Faroe Islands, except parts of paras. 4 and 5. Within para. 4, pharmacies and promotion of health (environmental issues) have been taken over as matters of the Faroe Islands, while the rest of the health area is still a common matter where framework legislation is enacted by the Parliament of Denmark, but particular legal rules and administration is with the authorities of the Faroe Islands to the extent subsidies from the state budget are paid to the Faroe Islands. Within para. 5, social care, mandatory insurance for accidents, labour force, labour relations, apprenticeships and vacations have been taken over as matters of the Faroe Islands, while special forms of social care and general social insurance are still common matters where framework legislation is enacted by the Parliament of Denmark, but particular legal rules and administration is with the authorities of the Faroe Islands to the extent subsidies from the state budget are paid to the Faroe Islands.

Over the years, several of these matters have been transferred from the Parliament of Denmark to the Legislative Assembly of the Faroe Islands.[13]

A portion of competences mentioned in both List A and List B are still with the Danish Parliament. Both lists feature mainly fields of law or matters that are of a public law nature. Thus, the original distribution of legislative powers concerning the Faroe Islands seems to have left the area of private law almost entirely in the hands of the Parliament of Denmark, as well as criminal law and legislation dealing with courts and the law of procedure.

From 2005, the distribution of legislative powers in principle starts from the position that the Legislative Assembly of the Faroe Islands can, by means of its own legislative decisions, transfer legislative competence from the Parliament of Denmark to the Legislative Assembly of the Faroe Islands for the purpose of law-making within the territory of the Faroe Islands.[14] The 2005 Takeover Act divides the legislative competence of the Parliament of Denmark into three categories, namely matters that cannot be transferred (see above), matters that can be transferred after negotiations between the governments of Denmark and the Faroe Islands, and matters that can be transferred without negotiations. The second category of matters, that is, those that under Section 2(2) of the 2005 Takeover Act can be transferred after negotiations, contains elements of both public law and private law. In the field of public law, this category contains the following: functions as legal counsel; the established church; industrial property rights (i.e., patents and trademarks); care of offenders; air traffic; passports; police and prosecutors and those parts of criminal law that are connected to them; the administration of justice (including the establishment of courts of law); criminal law; aliens' affairs; border control. In the field of private law, the category contains the following: property; industrial property rights (other than decision-making on patents and trade marks); family law and inheritance law; and the law of persons.[15] Although negotiations are prescribed for the transfer of certain matters, the purpose of such negotiations is not to give the Danish government a possibility to stop the transfer, but rather to ensure that such transfer is well managed and that it takes place in good order.

Although there exist broad possibilities to transfer legislative competence to the Faroe Islands and although many matters have been transferred from the Danish

[13]For examples of such areas of law that were not mentioned in any of the lists but that were discussed for the purposes of legislative action in the Faroe Islands (mortgaging of cargo, working environment of state authorities in the Faroe Islands, names of persons, safety at sea), see Rasmussen 2002, pp. 377–380.

[14]According to Section 46 of the 1994 Faroese Act on the Government of the Faroe Islands, after the decision of the government of the Faroe Islands, a matter is overtaken pursuant to an act of the Legislative Assembly. See also Forslag til Lov om de færøske myndigheders overtagelse af sager og sagsområder, fremsat den 11. maj 2005 af statsministeren (Anders Fogh Rasmussen), where it is mentioned in sub-section 3.2. that the authorities of the Faroe Islands make particular decisions about taking over legislative competence.

[15]See Forslag til Lov om de færøske myndigheders overtagelse af sager og sagsområder, fremsat den 11. maj 2005 af statsministeren (Anders Fogh Rasmussen), section 2 on main points of the proposal.

Parliament to the Legislative Assembly of the Faroe Islands, there still exist competences with the Danish Parliament which, although they are transferable, have not been transferred. The system of distribution of competence in the 2005 Takeover Act creates a procedure by means of which the Faroese law-maker transfers competences from the Danish Parliament to itself on the basis of its own legislative decisions. This leads to the result that different parts of the legislative competence of the Faroe Islands are established in a number of different pieces of Faroese legislation that have been enacted at different points in time. As a consequence, the system appears fragmented and is difficult to comprehend from a general point of view.[16] As concerns the division of the legal order between public law and private law, it is clear that the Faroese law-maker could, in theory, have complete powers not only within the sphere of private law, but also within most parts of public law, except in those areas reserved to the Parliament of Denmark under Section 1(2) of the Takeover Act.

Seemingly in order to establish which competences still remain with the Danish Parliament, the Legislative Assembly of the Faroe Islands enacted on 10 May 2006 a particular Faroese Act in which were listed all 24 competences that had not at that point in time been transferred from the Danish Parliament to the Faroese Legislative Assembly but that could be transferred (and which, as a consequence, are not featured in the enumeration of matters that according to Section 1(2) of the 2005 Takeover Act belong to the Danish Parliament).[17] According to this Faroese Act, in May 2006, the Parliament of Denmark held the following competences that were subject to the requirement of negotiation before transfer on the basis of Section 2(2) of the 2009 Takeover Act: functions of legal counsel; industrial property rights (such as patents and trademarks); the established church; property; care of offenders; air traffic; passports; family law and inheritance law and the law of persons; police and prosecutors and those parts of the criminal law that are connected to them; the administration of justice (including the establishment of courts of law); and criminal law. The matters still held by the Parliament in 2006 that could be transferred without negotiations to the Legislative Assembly were the following: emergency services; religious communities deviating from the established church; holidays; financial institutions and their supervision; general retirement pensions; geological surveys; meteorology; weights and measures; copyright; company law; health, regulation of medical doctors and midwives, and hospitals; care of the disabled; pilotage within the law of the sea, marking of fairways, lighthouses; and alien affairs and border control. Both categories contain legislative competences that fall into both spheres of the legal order, public law and private law.

---

[16]See, e.g., Rasmussen 2017, pp. 60–65.

[17]Løgtingslóg nr. 41 frá 10. mai 2006 um ræði á málum og málsøkjum, sum seinast broytt við løgtingslóg nr. 55 frá 26. mai 2011, at http://www.logir.fo/Logtingslog/41-fra-10-05-2006-um-raedi-a-malum-og-malsokjum-sum-seinast-broytt-vid-logtingslog (accessed on 4 January 2018).

Since the enactment of the Faroese Act in 2006, legislative competences have several times been transferred from the Parliament to the Legislative Assembly. For instance, transfer of competence within the heading "criminal law" took place such that the governments of Denmark and the Faroe Islands first gave a joint declaration on 15 May 2009 as to what the delicts, punishments and other criminal sanctions are and what the preconditions are for a finding of guilt. In addition, according to the declaration the two parties pledge to closely cooperate within the area of criminal law after the transfer of competence, in particular with a view to ensuring that there will, in Denmark and the Faroe Islands, exist a similar respect for the core fundamental values and principles present in the judicial and legislative tradition. As a consequence, the Legislative Assembly enacted on 17 February 2010 an Act that amended the Faroese Act of 2006 listing the competences held by the Danish Parliament, in which the heading "criminal law" was deleted from the list of powers of the Danish Parliament.[18]

In this way, by making a negative decision concerning the Parliament's competence in the area of criminal law, the Legislative Assembly defined its own legislative competence within the area. It is perhaps debatable whether this decision moves towards enumeration of Faroese competences or towards a residual competence (in which case the Faroe Islands would develop a more federal model of distribution of legislative powers). In any event, the 2005 Takeover Act formulates the approach by reference to positive determination of transfer of competence leading to a piecemeal enumeration of Faroese competences. Further, the enumerations established pursuant to the 1948 Home Rule Act for the Faroe Islands appear to result in a Faroese enumeration of law-making matters. There is a condition to the taking over of matters and fields of law, expressed in the *travaux preparatoires* to the Takeover Act, namely that the entire matter has to be taken over by the Faroe Islands, not only a part thereof.[19]

Other legislative matters that have been taken over are: media matters; emergency services; the established church and religious communities that deviate from the established church; matters that concern company law, economic associations and foundations as well as annual accounts (book-keeping); holidays; weights and measures; meteorology; copyright; property; criminal law; and pilotage.[20] This

[18]Løgtingslóg nr. 7 frá 17. februar 2010 um broyting í løgtingslóg um ræði á málum og málsøkjum, at http://www.logir.fo/Logtingslog/7-fra-17-02-2010-um-broyting-i-logtingslog-um-raedi-a-malum-og-malsokjum (accessed on 12 January 2018), dealt with the repeal of Section 1, Sub-section 2, para. 15 of the Faroese Act of 2006 with the listing of Danish powers.

[19]Forslag til Lov om de færøske myndigheders overtagelse af sager og sagsområder, fremsat den 11. maj 2005 af statsministeren (Anders Fogh Rasmussen), section 3.2.2. For a specification of the contents of each matter or field of law from the point of view of material Danish law that has been passed within the matter, see sections 3.2.2.1.–3.2.2.12.

[20]See the 2014 report of the State Commissioner on the Faroe Islands (Rigsombudsmanden på Færøerne—Beretning 2014), p. 223, at http://www.stm.dk/Index/mainstart.asp/multimedia/Beretning_2014_PDF1.pdf (accessed on 16 October 2015). See also an English-language version of the list of matters taken over by the Faroe Islands at http://stm.dk/multimedia/FO_UK_oversigt_sagsomraader_010811.pdf (accessed on 20 October 2015).

means that significant legislative matters, such as health, practice as a medical doctor, practice as a midwife, and hospitals as well as care of the disabled still remain within the competence of the Danish Parliament, although they could be transferred. However, because transfer of competence also means transfer of financial responsibility, future transfers are very dependent on what the Faroese economy is capable of funding from its own budget.

It is not, however, self-evident that transfer of legislative competence will always take place according to the political plan, as is evidenced by the functions of legal counsel, concerning which the Minister of Justice of Denmark and the Minister of Internal Affairs of the Faroe Islands signed a joint declaration on 15 May 2009. A bill to was submitted to the Legislative Assembly, but when the proposal to transfer competence concerning the functions of legal counsel was dealt with in the Legislative Assembly, the lawyers of the Faroe Islands commenced a broad campaign against the transfer. As a consequence, the Legislative Assembly declined the bill of the government of the Faroe Islands and decided against transfer within this area of legal competence.

A further issue is whether or not it is possible to transfer legislative powers from the Legislative Assembly of the Faroe Islands to the Parliament of Denmark. This kind of reversal of the competences of the Faroe Islands is not foreseen in the 2005 Takeover Act, which tends to indicate that such reverse transfer would only be possible on the basis of an agreement between the Government of Denmark and the Government of the Faroe Islands, followed by a legislative decision concerning reversal in the Faroe Islands, ending with an amendment of the 2005 Takeover Act, where such an area of law or matter could be placed.

In addition, the Faroe Islands has been granted a limited measure of international competence to conclude treaties under public international law on the basis of the 2005 Act on the Treaty Competence of the Government of the Faroe Islands.[21] This Act establishes a precondition for the exercise of such treaty powers that the matter dealt with in the treaty belongs to the legislative competence of the Faroe Islands and that Denmark as a State has not exercised its treaty competence concerning the same matter. In the final instance, however, Denmark as a State is liable for any such international obligations that the Faroe Islands have assumed. The main principle under Section 5 of the 1948 Home Rule Act is that "[t]he competence of the Faroese authorities is subject to the limitation caused by treaty rights and to other international rights and obligations existing at any time. In matters concerning the relation of the Kingdom to foreign countries the decision lies with the State authorities." Therefore, if an act of the Legislative Assembly is in violation of an international treaty that Denmark has concluded and that is applicable in the Faroe

---

[21]Lov nr. 579 af 24. Juni 2005 om Færøernes landsstyres indgåelse af folkeretlige aftaler. For an English-language version of this Act, see http://stm.dk/_p_13089.html (accessed on 4 January 2018).

Islands, the act is invalid.[22] In this sense, the general treaty powers of Denmark could in principle put the Faroe Islands in a similar situation to that of the Åland Islands under the 1920 Self-Government Act, when leakage of competence from Åland to Finland was perceived as a problem.

As has been seen above, the enumerations of the legislative powers of the sub-state levels in the three states, Canada, Denmark and Finland, are broad in nature and empower the sub-state levels to regulate the behaviour of individuals and legal persons within their territories. The possibility of transferring legislative powers from the Danish Parliament to the Legislative Assembly of the Faroe Islands seems to establish an opt-out regime by which the Faroe Islands can decide to opt out from national legislation.[23] From the point of view of international law, in particular human rights law, law-making powers at the sub-state level turn the relevant sub-state entities into the State at the same time as the responsibilities of the State under international law are carried by the States themselves.[24]

---

[22]See, e.g., Preliminary answers to questions raised by the Guernsey Constitutional Investigation Committee, Prime Minister's Office, Faroe Islands, 28 October 2014, para. 12 (on file with the author). See also the decree of the Danish Government on the entering into force of the European Convention of Human Rights in the Faroe Islands (Anordning nr. 136 af 25. Februar 2000 om ikrafttræden for Færøerne af lov om Den Europæiske Menneskerettighedskonvention), at http://logir.fo/Anordning/136-af-25-02-2000-om-ikrafttraeden-for-Faeroerne-af-lov-om-Den-Europaeiske-Menneskerettighedskonvention (accessed on 10 November 2015).

[23]See Hogg 2014, s. 5.1(d), where the difficulties posed for the federal parliament of the operation of a general opt-out scheme are commented, at the same time as some examples on such national policies are given from which the province of Quebec has opted out (although when doing so, not opting out from any of the federal powers established in Section 91 of the Constitution). See also Hogg 2014, s. 6.7 for examples of opting-out.

[24]On the relationship between sub-state entities in Canada and Finland, on the one hand, and international human rights treaties, see *Ekholm v. Finland*, Application no. 68050/01, European Court of Human Rights, Judgment of 24 July 2007 (in which Finland was found to be in violation for non-application in the Åland Islands by Ålandic public authorities of legislation within the competence of Åland, amounting to failure to comply with domestic judicial decisions), *Ballantyne, Davidson, McIntyre v. Canada*, Communications Nos. 359/1989 and 385/1989 to the UN Human Rights Committee, U.N. Doc. CCPR/C/47/D/359/1989 and 385/1989/Rev.1 (1993) (where a violation of freedom of expression in Art. 19 CCPR was found on the part of Canada for legislation in Quebec on banning public display of advertisements in English), and *Waldman v. Canada*, Communication No 694/1996 to the UN Human Rights Committee, meeting of 3 November 1999, U.N.Doc. CCPR/C/67/D/694/1996 (where a violation of equality in Art. 26 CCPR was found on the part of Canada for legislation in Ontario that made possible public funding to Roman Catholic schools, but not to other private denominational schools). It appears that for the time being, no individual case has been resolved before any treaty body that would involve the application of the law of the Faroe Islands. Concerning the position of Canada to international law, see also *Ahani v. Canada*, (2002) 58 O.R. (3d) 107 (C.A.); leave to appeal to the S.C.C. denied on May 16, 2002, as commented in Hogg 2014, s. 11.4(a), the case of *Labour Conventions*, [1937] A.C. 326, 349, as commented in Hogg 2014, s. 11.5(b), 11.5(c), and the *Radio Reference*, [1932] A.C. 304, 312, as commented in Hogg 2014, s. 11.5(c). It seems that position of the Faroe Islands in relation to international law is the opposite also to the Canadian situation, and that applicability of international law is apparently dependent on whether the Legislative Assembly has been presented the international treaty.

3.4 Limited or No Existence of Concurrent Powers

In principle, the vast bulk of legislative powers of the federation and the provinces in Canada are exclusive in relation to each other and do not overlap with each other to produce concurrent powers that could compete over the right to legislate on a certain matter (although the evolution of the interpretation of constitutional law through courts indicates adjustments to this main principle by means of concurrent *application*; see Sect. 4.2.1). However, in some particular instances outside of Sections 91 and 92, which in principle do not produce any overlap, concurrent powers do exist.

In Section 92A, there is an explicit concurrent jurisdiction between the federation and the provinces. According to para. 2 of the Section, "in each province, the legislature may make laws in relation to the export from the province to another part of Canada of the primary production from non-renewable natural resources and forestry resources in the province and the production from facilities in the province for the generation of electrical energy, but such laws may not authorize or provide for discrimination in prices or in supplies exported to another part of Canada". Para. 3 of the same section continues by stating that "nothing in subsection (2) derogates from the authority of Parliament to enact laws in relation to the matters referred to in that subsection and, where such a law of Parliament and a law of a province conflict, the law of Parliament prevails to the extent of the conflict". In para. 6 of the Section, there is a limitation of derogation with respect to powers enjoyed by the provinces on the basis of their own legislative competences prior to the entering into force of the constitutional provision in 1982, fashioned in a manner that circumscribes the powers of the federal parliament. Further within the sphere of public law, concerning the provinces of Ontario, Nova Scotia, and New Brunswick, the Parliament of Canada has the unrestricted power, under Section 94, to make provision for the uniformity of all or any of the laws relating to the procedure of all or any of the courts in those three states. However, such uniformity law shall not have any effect in any province unless the provincial legislature also enacts it as law.[25] As pointed out above, such doubling of the law-making procedure for the entering into force of an Act appears to be a stricter requirement than the requirement of consent in the context of the Åland Islands.

According to Section 94A, the Parliament of Canada may make laws in relation to old age pensions and supplementary benefits, including survivors' and disability benefits irrespective of age, but provinces also have that power. As pointed out (see Sect. 3.1), in this area there is an interesting inverted supremacy clause in operation,

---

[25]This provision is rarely used in courts. However, see *Reference re Assisted Human Reproduction Act*, [2010] 3 SCR 457, 2010 SCC 61 (CanLII), which dealt with the constitutionality of various provisions in the federal Assisted Human Reproduction Act. The Act was in part upheld (especially as concerns the criminalizations), but in part unconstitutional, because some of the provisions crossed over to the provincial powers and could not be saved, e.g., by reference to ancillary powers.

because no such law enacted by the Parliament shall affect the operation of any law present or future of a provincial legislature in relation to any such matter. Therefore, a provincial law-maker may pass legislation that derogates from federal law in this area and sets aside federal law. This is a unique feature of Canadian federalism in comparison with other federations and turns the classical federal preemption constellations upside down.

Moreover, according to Section 95, agriculture in the province and immigration into the province is, in principle and originally, a legislative competence of the province. However, as pointed out (see Sect. 3.1), the Parliament of Canada is also empowered to make laws in relation to agriculture in all or any of the provinces, and to immigration into all or any of the provinces, which means that with respect to these matters, there is completely concurrent jurisdiction.

As mentioned above, the spheres of legislative competence of the Åland Islands, on the one hand, and the Parliament of Finland, on the other, are exclusive in relation to each other and based on the enumeration of powers. The lists of legislative competence are perceived as a more or less complete demarcation of the two legislative competencies, but reference is made at the end of both enumerations to "other matters" that are deemed to be within the legislative power of the Legislative Assembly or of the Parliament of Finland according to the principles underlying the Self-Government Act, indicating that for matters which are difficult to allocate through the listing of express competences, the question of competence may be resolved on the basis of a principle of affinity (see Chap. 5).[26]

According to section 18(27), the legislative competence of the Legislative Assembly comprises matters other than those listed in section 18 if deemed to be within the legislative power of Åland in accordance with the principles underlying the Self-Government Act, while section 27(42) makes reference to other matters that are deemed to be within the legislative power of the Parliament of Finland according to the principles underlying the Act. The provisions can be said to constitute implied powers for both the Legislative Assembly and the Parliament of Finland, but they have not been invoked to any great extent.[27] In spite of this abstract extension at the end of both enumerations, the point of departure is that the two enumerations do not, in principle, produce any situations where both law-makers would be competent to exercise their law-making powers at the same time for the jurisdiction of the Åland Islands.

The situation is in principle similar in the Faroe Islands, that is, that there is no area of concurrent powers since the 2005 Takeover Act. The short list of matters not transferable from the Danish Parliament and the Faroese listing of matters that have been transferred nevertheless seems to leave an intermediate area of law where matters have not yet been transferred. As a consequence, they can be regarded as "joint" matters, which appears to be the position under Section 6(1) of the 1948

[26]For an example, see the Opinion of the Supreme Court No. 3169 of 9 October 1994 concerning the holding of an advisory EU referendum, Chap. 5.

[27]See Suksi 2005, p. 242 ff.

Home Rule Act. This is, however, not a true overlap, because the Danish Parliament holds those legislative powers on the basis of Section 9 of the 1948 Home Rule Act until they have been formally transferred by the Legislative Assembly of the Faroe Islands, which means they are general legislative powers of the Danish Parliament under Section 3 of the Constitution of Denmark.[28] Within this area of transferable but not yet transferred matters of a common nature, common to the Realm, the Danish Parliament has enacted framework legislation which makes it possible for the governmental authorities of the Faroe Islands to pass implementing norms applicable to the Faroe Islands.[29] This is the case, for instance, in the area of health (see Sect. 3.3). Within those delegated powers, the Faroe Islands is entitled to pass specifying norms and is also entitled to subsidies from the Danish state budget for the public functions thus exercised on behalf of Denmark proper.[30]

As the review of concurrent powers in three constitutional settings shows, the exclusive nature of the two orders of enumerated powers in each country in principle creates a sharp competence line between the two areas of law. This competence line is to some extent blurred in Canada by an overlap of federal and provincial legislative powers in certain areas (natural resources, forestry resources and electrical energy; old age pensions and supplementary benefits, including survivors' and disability benefits irrespective of age, agriculture, and immigration), but in the main and in principle, it should in almost all instances be clear who the holder of law-making powers is in respect to any given matter. In Canada, the competence line is, however, less marked than the text of the Constitution indicates.

3.5 Lack of Federal or National Supremacy

Because, formally, concurrent powers appear to be few in the three countries to the point of being non-existent in Finland and potentially also in Denmark, situations should rarely arise in which national law would have to supersede sub-state law. This distinguishes the three cases reviewed here from regular federalism, where a supremacy clause is explicitly provided for, for instance, in Article VI, clause 2, of the US Constitution and section 31 of the Basic Law of Germany and where a preemption doctrine (at least in the US) seems to permit ever broader incursions into the legislative powers of the constituent states. Lack of federal or national

---

[28]See also Rasmussen 2002, p. 377.

[29]See, e.g., Lov nr 316 af 17/05/1995 om om sundhedsvæsenet på Færøerne, at http://www.sslug.dk/~chlor/www.retsinformation.dk/lov/l46921.html (accessed on 10 November 2015). This Act of the Danish Parliament grants the power to the Government of the Faroe Islands to pass rules about the services, benefits and administration of health issues, and it also grants the Legislative Assembly the right to amend provisions of the national health legislation, except certain provisions of the national Hospitals Act.

[30]See, e.g., speech by Eidesgaard (2006).

supremacy is therefore indicative of wide powers of the sub-state entities typical of autonomy arrangements.[31]

In principle, there is little supremacy principle or preemption doctrine present in the Canadian Constitution,[32] and where it exists, it does so in somewhat surprising ways. First and foremost, there is no explicit supremacy clause in the Canadian Constitution that would give ordinary federal law in general a preemptive role or a primacy in relation to provincial legislation (but nonetheless a certain paramountcy doctrine has been developed in court practice; see Sect. 4.2.1). However, some specific areas of law mentioned in the Constitution do contain explicit mechanisms of supremacy.

As concerns concurrent powers in the area of natural resources, forestry resources and electrical energy established in Section 92A, a relatively narrow material area of concurrent powers, there is a supremacy clause in operation that gives preeminence to federal legislation in situations of conflict. In addition, under Section 94A, the Parliament of Canada may make laws in relation to old age pensions and supplementary benefits, including survivors' and disability benefits irrespective of age. However, as pointed out (see Sects. 3.1 and 3.4), there is an inverted supremacy clause in operation here, because no such law shall affect the operation of any law present or future of a provincial legislature in relation to any such matter. Therefore, a provincial law-maker may pass legislation that derogates from federal law in this area and sets aside federal law so as to effect a provincial preemption within the area of these social benefits.[33]

A more regular federal preemption is created under Section 95, according to which agriculture in the province and immigration into the province are, in principle and originally, a legislative competence of the province. However, the Parliament

---

[31]Suksi 2011, p. 127 f.

[32]As pointed out in Hogg 2014, s. 15.9(d), "[t]hese three provisions [sections 92A(2) and 92A(3), 94A, 95—MS] obviously cover only a small portion of the field of legislative power. In the Canadian scheme of distribution, exclusivity is the rule and concurrency the exception". Hogg contrasts the Canadian situation to the situation in the USA and Australia, but is of the opinion that the difference is in practice not as sharp as one might expect.

[33]See *Hislop v. Canada (Attorney General)*, 2009 ONCA 354 (CanLII), in which the Canada Pension Plan was held to be valid federal legislation, enacted Section 94A, while Class Proceedings Act, 1992, under which claims for crediting remuneration towards pensions were made, was valid provincial legislation enacted under Section 92(13, 14) as procedural law which neither modified nor created substantive rights to pension. The power that Section 94A confers on Parliament to make laws in relation to old age pensions and supplementary benefits is expressly concurrent with provincial power over the same subject-matter and sets up a reverse paramountcy rule, assigning predominance to provincial laws contrary to the usual preferential place accorded to federal laws. To engage Section 94A, there must be both federal and provincial laws in relation to old age pensions and supplementary benefits, or laws in relation to either one of those subjects. The Court held that the CPP qualifies as a law in relation to old age pensions and supplementary benefits but that the CPA cannot claim any such constitutional foundation. The CPA is a statute of general application, a law that deals with procedure in civil matters, but is not and does not purport to be a law in relation to old age pensions and supplementary benefits. Therefore, the conditions under which establishing provincial paramountcy could have emerged were not established.

of Canada is also empowered to make laws in relation to agriculture in all or any of the provinces, and regarding immigration into all or any of the provinces, which means that with respect to these matters, there is a completely concurrent jurisdiction. As a consequence (see Sect. 3.1), there is an explicit preemption principle in the area of federal legislation concerning agriculture and immigration, stating that any provincial law on the same matter shall have effect in and for the province as long and as far only as it is not in conflict with any Act of the Parliament of Canada.

The conclusion that the legislative powers of the Åland Islands are exclusive in relation to the powers of the Parliament of Finland means that the Parliament of Finland cannot, by its own enactments, fill a normative void within the competence sphere of the Legislative Assembly. Nor can the authorities of the Åland Islands use legislation from the competence sphere of the Parliament of Finland as a legal basis for their decisions to fill a normative void within the competence sphere of the Åland Islands.[34]

This is confirmed in a number of cases by the Supreme Administrative Court. For instance, in SAC 2003:1, the Court concluded that in the absence of a provision concerning the self-rectification of an administrative decision in legislation of the Åland Islands, the Government of the Åland Islands could not, by means of a decision of its own, carry out such a self-rectification, and the provision in the Administration Act applicable in mainland Finland could not be applied. In SAC 1982-A-II-1, the Court stated that provisions which in mainland Finland were included in an Act concerning the steering of agricultural production had not been enacted in the Åland Islands within the legislative competence of the Legislative Assembly. Therefore, corresponding steering measures could not be undertaken in the Åland Islands. Thus in concrete instances, the parallel existence of the two legal orders is based on mutual exclusivity, which does not permit the use in one jurisdiction of norms that belong to the other jurisdiction. The incapacity of the Parliament of Finland to enact legislation for the Åland Islands within the legislative competences of the Legislative Assembly hence means in effect that the national Parliament cannot act on the basis of any principle of preemption in relation to the Åland Islands when enacting ordinary legislation.

Although the Legislative Assembly may exercise its legislative powers within the enumerated area designated for the Åland Islands, it does not have a general obligation to do so in relation to each matter established in the list.[35] Insofar as the Legislative Assembly has chosen not to adopt a norm that regulates a specific issue, it cannot be expected or compelled to do so, except in three situations. An expectation of enactment of legislation follows from the regulatory tasks that the Constitution of Finland places upon the lawmaker, in particular, in the constitutional rights established in chapter 2 of the Constitution. Therefore, it could be

[34]See also Palmgren 1995, p. 88.

[35]However, see Jääskinen 2003, p. 16, who is of the opinion that the Åland Islands has, on the basis of the general foundational solutions in the Self-Government Act, a duty to legislate within areas that belong to the legislative competence of the Åland Islands if a non-regulated situation is considered unacceptable.

argued that there are constitutional rights that require legislative action by the Legislative Assembly in particular in the area of the economic, social and cultural rights as well as in the area of the environment. Also, the Self-Government Act contains provisions that require the Legislative Assembly to enact certain acts of Åland, such as section 7(3) concerning particular grounds for granting regional citizenship, section 8(2) on the loss of regional citizenship in some cases, section 15 on the right of the Legislative Assembly to dissolve itself and call new elections, section 16 on the procedure for appointing the Government of the Åland Islands, and section 24(1) on the possibility to appoint individuals other than Nordic citizens to public office. A third category of obligation to legislate in the Ålandic sphere of legislative competence is where EU law takes the form of a directive which does not find any other normative channel of implementation than an act of Åland.[36] However, the obligation of the Legislative Assembly to legislate in these areas does not constitute an issue of supremacy or preemption on the part of the exercise of legislative powers of the Parliament of Finland, but follows from duties established in constitutional legislation (application of the Constitution in the

---

[36]Initially, the Supreme Court held in an Opinion from 1997 that it would not include implementation of EU law in the Åland Islands in the control of legislative competence, but this position was reversed. The changed position is present in, e.g., Opinion of 18 August 2003 (Dnr 1958), where the Supreme Court held that a violation of legislative competence has taken place when the Ålandic Tobacco Act did not correctly implement Section 8 of the Tobacco Directive of the EU. The Supreme Court is, however, of the opinion that the review of Ålandic Acts in relation to EU law is not performed in a comprehensive manner by the Supreme Court, but is in practice dependent on regular mechanism of preliminary rulings from the Court of Justice of the European Union, effectuated when courts of law apply the Ålandic legislation in concrete situations, alternatively in proceedings instituted by the European Commission against Finland in the Court of Justice for breach of treaty-based obligations. In the context of competence control, implementation of EU directives has recently been mentioned, albeit not fashioned as violation of the competence of the Parliament, in, e.g., Opinion of the Supreme Court of 31 March 2017 (Dnr OH 2017/34; Directive 2014/30/EU of the European Parliament and of the Council of 26 February 2014 on the harmonisation of the laws of the Member States relating to electromagnetic compatibility and Directive 2014/35/EU of the European Parliament and of the Council of 26 February 2014 on the harmonisation of the laws of the Member States relating to the making available on the market of electrical equipment designed for use within certain voltage limits) and Opinion of 12 September 2017 (Dnr OH 2017/133; Directive 2014/61/EU of the European Parliament and of the Council of 15 May 2014 on measures to reduce the cost of deploying high-speed electronic communications networks). In the Opinion of 31 March 2017 (Dnr OH 2017/33; Directive 2014/33/EU of the European Parliament and of the Council of 26 February 2014 on the harmonisation of the laws of the Member States relating to lifts and safety components for lifts), the Supreme Court summarized the praxis by concluding that provisions in Ålandic acts have been vetoed if it has been evident that they would lead to a conflict between the legislation of the EU and legislation of the Åland Islands. This was the case at least in relation to legislation concerning emissions trade (OH 2005/61) and prevention of discrimination (OH 2005/91). Following that praxis, the Supreme Court recommended to the President that two provisions in the Ålandic Act on Implementing the State Act on Safety of Elevators be vetoed for breach of Section 27(4) concerning the legislative competence of the State in the area of foreign relations.

Åland Islands,[37] unless excepted in the 1991 Self-Government Act) or from the supremacy of EU law (which would, in particular, affect matters such as agriculture, fisheries, environment, etc.).

Ålandic membership of the EU means that the legislative powers of the Åland Islands are delimited by EU law. It is inherent in the nature of EU law that it sets aside any conflicting national law, irrespective of the normative status of the latter. This means that there is an EU supremacy doctrine or preemption doctrine at work in relation to the legislative powers of the Åland Islands in a manner which is not very different from a regular federal situation. The Åland Islands are autonomous in relation to mainland Finland, but just as non-autonomous in relation to the EU and EU law as any Member State of the EU, because of the primacy of EU law. For the individual or business enterprise, this means that three legislators have competence to pass legislation within the area of the Åland Islands: that of the Åland Islands, that of Finland, and that of the EU, and it is not always easy to know which one to follow.[38]

Matters are different in the Faroe Islands, which is not a part of the EU although Denmark is a Member State. Here, no supremacy of EU law works to create a preemption principle, which means that the only relevant relationship is that between the Danish Parliament and the Legislative Assembly of the Faroe Islands. In this relationship, the competence line is again in principle sharp, with no possibility that the exclusive competences of Faroe Islands would be infringed by ordinary legislative enactments of the Danish Parliament. Of course, the Danish Constitution applies in the Faroe Islands, with those exceptions introduced by the 1948 Home Rule Act and the 2005 Takeover Act.

---

[37]See Suksi 2005, p. 469, for a listing of provisions of the Constitution that apply in the Åland Islands, of provisions of the Constitution whose applicability on the Åland Islands is excepted by the Self-Government Act, and of provisions whose applicability is unclear. Notably, the Opinions of the Supreme Court relatively often deal with Section 121 of the Constitution when Ålandic legislation is enacted within the legislative competence of the Åland Islands with a view to municipal law. In such situations of applicability of Section 121 of the Constitution, which is clear, the Supreme Court asks whether the Ålandic legislation respects the constitutional right of self-government accorded to municipalities, in particular in light of the praxis on the same issue of the Constitutional Committee of the Parliament of Finland. See, e.g., Opinions of 16 December 2015 (OH2015/213; within competence), 12 September 2017 (OH2017/135; not within competence).

[38]See the Supreme Court case SC 2004:65 on a damages claim towards the Government of the Åland Islands by a fisherman, in which the relationship between the three jurisdictions, the European Union, Finland and the Åland Islands, is worked out. According to the case, a fisherman involved in commercial fishing of salmon in the Åland Islands should have followed the quota provisions of an EU regulation, not those of the national Ministry of Agriculture and Forestry and certainly not those of the Government of the Åland Islands for reasons of *ultra vires* creation of individual fishing quotas in the Åland Islands. See also the case SC 2017:47, where the Supreme Court held that lacking agreement between governmental authorities of Finland and the Åland Islands on the distribution of a fishing quota allocated to Finland by the EU, the national Ministry of Agriculture and Forestry was competent to determine the distribution of the quota between mainland Finland and the Åland Islands.

The three countries display a similarity with exclusive powers both at the national and the sub-state levels. Some relatively limited competence areas in Canada are concurrent, but as a rule the Canadian Constitution communicates *prima facie* a principle of watertight compartments between the federal and the provincial level. As we shall see below, that is not the position taken in constitutional interpretation in Canada. Also, it is not always the case that federal law has supremacy: provincial law can also be given supremacy in Canada. Perhaps Canada, in addition to being a federation, also is a country of autonomies. The Åland Islands and the Faroe Islands are immune from the supremacy of national law, but the Åland Islands, which belong to the European Union, nonetheless face an EU primacy rule.

References

Barnett H (2010) Understanding public law. Routledge-Cavendish, London, New York

Craik N, Forcese C, Bryden P, Carver P, Haigh R, Ratushny Ed, Sullivan R (eds) (2011) Public law—cases, materials, and commentary, 2nd edn. Emond Montgomery Publications, Toronto

Eidesgaard J (2006) 'Færøernes forfatningsmæssige stilling', speech at Nordic Lawyers' Academy on 24 August 2006 in Tórshavn, the Faroe Islands (on file with author)

Forslag til Lov om de færøske myndigheders overtagelse af sager og sagsområder, fremsat den 11. maj 2005 af statsministeren

Hogg PW (2014) Constitutional law of Canada, 5th edn Supplemented, vols 1 and 2. Thomson & Carswell, Toronto [NB! References to Hogg 2014 are to sections in the supplemented loose-leaf volume, not to pages.]

Inwood GJ (2013) Understanding Canadian Federalism—an introduction to theory and practice. Pearson, Toronto

Jääskinen N (2003) EU: behörighet och Åland. Utredningsman Niilo Jääskinens utredning. Statsrådets kanslis publikationsserie 7/2003. Statsrådets kansli, Helsingfors

Le Sueur A, Sunkin M, Murkens JEK (2010) Public law—text, cases, and materials. Oxford University Press, Oxford

Leclair J (2010) "Please, draw me a field of jurisdiction": regulating securities, securing federalism. Supreme Court Law Rev 51(2):555

Palmgren S (1995) Landskapet Ålands lagstiftning. Nordisk Administrativt Tidsskrift 1:22–32

Rasmussen S (2002) Til hjemmestyreloven os skiller. Ugeskrift for Retsvæsen, nr. 43, 26 oktober 2002, pp 377–383

Rasmussen TV (2017) Opportunistisk dansk fortolkning af det færøske hjemmestyrets lovgivningskompetence. Ugeskrift for Retsvæsen, nr 6, februar 2017, pp 60–65

Suksi M (2005) Ålands konstitution. Åbo Akademis förlag, Åbo

Suksi M (2011) Sub-state governance through territorial autonomy. Springer, Heidelberg

Chapter 4
Management of Competence Claims

4.1 Bodies of Dispute Resolution

4.1.1 Canada: Symmetrical but Unsystematic Competence Control

In spite of careful delineation of national and sub-state competences in the enumerations of the fundamental documents, competence disputes will nonetheless arise in most countries with distribution of power provisions. For the resolution of such disputes, the fundamental documents may establish one or more mechanisms. Here, the focus will be on the main mechanisms in each country involved in the comparison, although some remarks will be also made concerning other mechanisms.

Under Section 56 of the Constitution of Canada, there is a power of disallowance in relation to federal law,[1] which is extended in Section 90 to provincial law.[2] Therefore, at least in theory, it would be possible to veto federal or provincial law that crosses over to the legislative competence of the other law-maker. However, this power of veto for the Governor General in relation to federal law or a Lieutenant

[1]"Where the Governor General assents to a Bill in the Queen's Name, he shall by the first convenient Opportunity send an authentic Copy of the Act to One of Her Majesty's Principal Secretaries of State, and if the Queen in Council within Two Years after Receipt thereof by the Secretary of State thinks fit to disallow the Act, such Disallowance (with a Certificate of the Secretary of State of the Day on which the Act was received by him) being signified by the Governor General, by Speech or Message to each of the Houses of the Parliament or by Proclamation, shall annul the Act from and after the Day of such Signification."

[2]"The following Provisions of this Act respecting the Parliament of Canada, namely—the Provisions relating to Appropriation and Tax Bills, the Recommendation of Money Votes, the Assent to Bills, the Disallowance of Acts, and the Signification of Pleasure on Bills reserved—shall extend and apply to the Legislatures of the several Provinces as if those Provisions were here re-enacted and made applicable in Terms to the respective Provinces and the Legislatures thereof, with the Substitution of the Lieutenant Governor of the Province for the Governor General, of the Governor General for the Queen and for a Secretary of State, of One Year for Two Years, and of the Province for Canada."

M. Suksi, *Double Enumeration of Legislative Powers in a Sub-State Context*, SpringerBriefs in Law, https://doi.org/10.1007/978-3-319-90921-9_4

Governor in relation to a provincial law has not been exercised since 1943 (although it was used relatively frequently up to and during the 1930s).[3] Therefore, although the formal provisions exist, it is possible to conclude that constitutionally, the mechanism has become a *desuetudo* on the basis of a constitutional convention and does not play any role in the resolution of competence claims.

For this reason, claims of exceeding legislative powers are only tried in courts of law and in the Supreme Court of Canada as the final instance. In the courts, which could be either provincial or federal, claims of unconstitutionality for reasons of violation of the distribution of powers can be brought by private claimants (such as individuals, NGOs) or by either the provinces or the federation. In this respect, courts of law can try the conformity with legislative competence of both the federal law-maker and the provincial law-makers, which means that the competence control is symmetrical and follows ordinary patterns of constitutional review on the basis of Section 52(1) of the Canadian Constitution. However, each and every piece of law passed by the federal parliament or a provincial legislature is not systematically checked for compliance with the distribution: possible violation of the distribution of competence arises primarily through individual cases.

This means that a piece of law or a provision that contains an unconstitutionality for reasons of violation of the legislative competence of another law-maker could stay in effect until a claim of unconstitutionality is tried and brought to a successful resolution either by lower courts or, on appeal from provincial courts of appeal or the federal court of appeal, by the Supreme Court of Canada. In making a decision of unconstitutionality in competence cases, the Court normally invalidates the entire act, and rarely invalidates only some parts of it so that those parts of the law that are not unconstitutional are not affected by the ruling. It is, however, possible for the Court to avoid invalidation on grounds of unconstitutionality by "reading down" the applicability of an act if its effects reach over the competence line to the other jurisdiction, so as to prevent its application in the other jurisdiction.[4] It is also possible under the Canadian system to request advisory opinions from the Supreme Court concerning draft acts. Several of the most important constitutional cases are, in fact, reference cases of this sort.[5]

4.1.2 Finland: Asymmetrical but Systematic Competence Control

Although the legislative competences of the Legislative Assembly of the Åland Islands and the Parliament of Finland are based on two separate enumerations, in practice only one of the enumerations is systematically checked for possible

[3]Hogg 2014, s. 5.3(e).

[4]Hogg 2014, ss. 15.6., 15.7.

[5]Hogg 2014, s. 8.6(a) and (b). See also Smith 2010, pp. 119–122.

transgressions, namely that of the Legislative Assembly of the Åland Islands. Each of the enactments of the Legislative Assembly is first scrutinized by the Åland Delegation,[6] and if problematic issues are detected, the Supreme Court is asked to deliver an opinion before the enactment is passed on to the President of Finland for the possible exercise of veto, either partial or total (since the introduction of partial veto in 1993, the total veto has rarely been used). This means that competence control is, in practice, performed in a one-dimensional manner, as if the Åland Islands were following the usual type of autonomy as a form of organization with residual powers at the national level, because enactments of the Parliament of Finland do not undergo the same systematic scrutiny for transgressions into the legislative competence of the Åland Islands.

In addition, the Parliament can easily break a presidential objection, which in this case is a weak suspensive veto, and possibly disregard the presidential warning of overstepping into the competence of Åland. However, despite the lack of systematic scrutiny, the Constitutional Committee of the Parliament of Finland considers itself competent to express itself *ante legem* on the compliance of draft laws before the Parliament of Finland with Section 27 of the 1991 Self-Government Act, that is, with the enumeration of the legislative powers of the Parliament of Finland within the territory of the Åland Islands. This rarely takes place, but the Constitutional Committee nonetheless sometimes gives opinions on whether the Bill is within the powers of the Parliament of Finland under Section 27. This adds a second dimension to competence control and makes it asymmetrical or more symmetrical instead of unilateral.

Under Section 19 of the Self-Government Act, the Åland Delegation, which is a joint body for different administrative and economic matters, also has a role in the determination of whether or not an act of Åland is within the competence of the Legislative Assembly as stipulated by Section 18 of the Act.[7] After the Legislative Assembly has made the decision on the adoption of an act of Åland, that decision is delivered both to the Ministry of Justice in the central government and to the Åland Delegation. The latter shall, according to Section 19, give its opinion to the former before the decision is presented to the President of the Republic by the Ministry of Justice. This opinion of the Åland Delegation is the first instance at which an external body exercises competence control, performed in two different ways: in respect of excess of powers and in respect of potential problems for the internal or external security of the state. If the Åland Delegation does not find any problems with the competence or security issues, the Ministry of Justice does not normally refer the matter to the Supreme Court for an opinion, but presents the act of Åland

[6]For a summary of review by the Åland Delegation concerning each Ålandic piece of law enacted between 1997 and 2007, see Ålandsdelegationen, XIII serien, åren 1997–2007, at https://www.ambetsverket.ax/sites/www.ambetsverket.ax/files/textsida_bilaga/ad_publikation_1997-2007_web.pdf (accessed on 5 February 2018). For more recent decisions of the Åland Delegation, see https://www.ambetsverket.ax/alandsdelegationen/arenden (accessed on 5 February 2018).

[7]For the decisions of the Åland Delegation (in Swedish), see http://www.ambetsverket.ax/alandsdelegationen/arenden (accessed on 3 November 2015).

to the President.[8] From the point of time when the Ålandic piece of law arrives at the Ministry of Justice, the President has a period of four months at her or his disposal to react to a competence problem in the enactment and inform the Government of the Åland Islands of her or his decision that there are obstacles to the entering into force of the act of Åland in full or in part. If the President does not react within four months,[9] the enactment is published by the Government of the Åland Islands in the Statutes of Åland, after which it enters into force on a day specified by the Government of the Åland Islands. As a rule, the President does not react negatively and veto Ålandic legislation which has not been flagged by the Åland Delegation and the Supreme Court for transgression of competence.

However, if the Åland Delegation does find a competence problem, or a vote in the Delegation indicates that there might be one, or if the matter decided by the Legislative Assembly is new or the issue is otherwise unclear on the basis of the Self-Government Act, the Ministry of Justice requests an opinion from the Supreme Court.[10] Such opinion of the Supreme Court is not a decision on an individual case concerning a real dispute between persons, but instead an abstract opinion *ante legem* about the application of Section 18 of the Self-Government Act,[11] perhaps in some ways comparable to the constitutional review performed in France by the *Conseil Constitutionnel* and in the UK by the Supreme Court in relation to Scottish legislation.[12] In addition, legislation relevant to the passing of the budget of the Åland Islands can be promulgated directly after adoption. In this case, competence control takes place *post legem* following the same procedure as described above. In such situation, the Supreme Court may also have to recommend to the President that the veto is used, this time with the effect of invalidating legislation or provisions thereof already in effect and in the process of implementation.

---

[8]See also Palmgren 1995, p. 89 f.

[9]As pointed out in Silverström 2008, p. 45, the waiting time due to the competence control may result in breaches of EU law because of incomplete implementation within the prescribed time, which may be shorter than the time reserved for competence control.

[10]See also Koskelo 2009, p. 11. However, Palmgren 1995, p. 91, remarks that in practice, "problems concerning the division of powers are usually solved by more or less informal consultations between the authorities". Such consultations probably takes place when prospective the enactment is still being formulated into a Bill of the Government of the Åland Islands or, at the latest, while the Bill is being dealt with by the Legislative Assembly.

[11]See Koskelo 2009, p. 13, who makes the personal reflection as the President of the Supreme Court that in this review, "it is not always easy to understand how the new law is intended to operate in practice".

[12]For the procedure of drafting of the opinions of the Supreme Court and making decisions on them in the Court, see Koskelo 2009, p. 12: "The matters are referred from the plenary meeting to a three-member committee and are then presented in a department consisting of five justices of the supreme court. The person presenting the matter assists in drafting the opinion at the committee and department stages. The committee's task is thus to do preparatory work and produce a draft opinion pending its final adoption at the department. The differences of opinion that sometimes arise generally become apparent already at the committee stage. If necessary, the opinion is put to a vote." For the Opinions of the Supreme Court (in Swedish), see http://www.korkeinoikeus.fi/sv/index/lausunnot/2009.html (accessed on 12 January 2018).

Opinions of the Supreme Court in matters of competence control in relation to the Åland Islands could be said to have binding status under customary law, because the President always follows these opinions,[13] although it has been pointed out in authoritative sources that the opinions of the Supreme Court do not bind the President.[14] However, there is no administrative or political discretion in the decision-making (except perhaps to the extent that the matter might deal with the internal or external security of the state, which is very rare). Instead, the President makes her or his decision on legal grounds as identified by the Supreme Court.[15] The President would not veto an Ålandic enactment, or parts of it, on the grounds that she or he felt the enactment was not in the interests of the Åland Islands or that the enactment was poorly drafted. This means that the veto powers of the President are not discretionary, although the system is to some extent fashioned in a way which is similar with the power of disallowance in the Canadian Constitution.

It is therefore primarily the review by the Supreme Court that carries the legal determination concerning particular enactments where there is an excess of

[13]Suksi 2005, p. 142. See also Koskelo 2009, p. 12, who concludes that to date, the president has followed the proposals of the Supreme Court and has generally also adopted the Court's reasoning.

[14]Koskelo 2009, p. 10. Koskelo was the President of the Supreme Court. According to her, the opinions of the Supreme Court serve as guidance, and although they are a prerequisite for a decision to exercise the veto, her opinion is that they are not binding. For such opinions, see also Suksi 2005, p. 141, Footnote. 52, where reference is made to the *travaux preparatoires* to the 1991 Self-Government Act. Therefore, in the face of continuous practice that normally would amount to a norm of a customary law nature, there are significant denials of the normative effect of such practice. See also Koskelo 2009, p. 12, for the comment that at least in one case dealing with an enactment of the Legislative Assembly that limited the right of certain officials to perform public duties in the Åland Islands, the President of Finland has not uncritically accepted the position of the Supreme Court. Instead, while not vetoing the enactment, she expressed her view on how the law should be applied so that it is in harmony with the Constitution. However, in a matter concerning public procurement, the interpretation of the competence line started with an Opinion from 1994, in which public procurement was deemed to be entirely within the competence of the Åland Islands. In 2007, when the Legislative Assembly passed new legislation on this matter, a majority of the Supreme Court said in its Opinion of 2 July 2007 (Dnr OH2007/75) that the dimension of competition law in the legislation had evolved to such an extent that the legislation was already to a great extent within the legislative competence of the Parliament of Finland on the basis of Section 27(10) of the Self-Government Act. The President nevertheless sided with the minority of the Supreme Court, which thought the legislation was still mainly about administrative procedure and as such within Ålandic competence on the basis of Section 18(1 and 4). As a consequence, the Ålandic law was not vetoed, but could enter into force, but the case can be presented as a rare exception to the rule that the President always follows the opinion of the Supreme Court (the fact that the Court was divided probably made it easier for the President to deviate from the Opinion). In 2017, further legislation in the area of public procurement was passed by the Legislative Assembly, but now the Supreme Court held that the legislation was within Ålandic competence. See Opinion of the Supreme Court, 12 September 2017 (Dnr OH2017/134).

[15]As pointed out by Koskelo 2009, p. 10, "the supreme court thus does not express an opinion on whether the legislation is appropriate or comment on the quality of the legislative product". Thus the Supreme Court of Finland would not give its legal opinion on the basis of the efficacy of the enactment of the Legislative Assembly.

competence on the part of the Legislative Assembly of the Åland Islands. In such situations, the Court identifies those provisions in the act that it finds fall outside the competence of the lawmaker of the Åland Islands. Three main categories of case appear in which the Supreme Court has had reason to propose that the President should exercise her veto: (1) the enactment of the Legislative Assembly is in breach of the Constitution of Finland[16]; (2) a provision in an enactment by the Legislative Assembly falls outside of the competence of the Åland Islands and thus remains within such a legislative matter that is within the enumerated competence of the Parliament of Finland[17]; and (3) the enactment of the Legislative Assembly is not in compliance with the legal norms of the European Union.[18] After having obtained an opinion from the Supreme Court the President of the Republic may, under Section 19(2), order the Ålandic enactment to be annulled in full or in part, if he or she considers that the Legislative Assembly has exceeded its legislative powers or that the enactment relates to the internal or external security of the state. The veto powers of the President in relation to an Ålandic enactment are therefore of an absolute nature, while the powers of the President in relation to the enactments of the Parliament of Finland are of a suspensive nature.

After the entering into force of the current Self-Government Act in 1993, it became possible for the President to use a partial veto, which means that it is not necessary to veto the entire Ålandic enactment if one provision is in breach of Ålandic competence. As a consequence of the reform, in almost all instances where the President has used the veto, the veto has been partial and dealt with only those provisions in the enactment that fell beyond the legislative competence of the Legislative Assembly.[19] Combined with the empirical fact that the President has

[16]According to Koskelo 2009, p. 11, these are generally minor, inadvertent infringements and deal, for instance, with the lack of constitutional authorization in the enactment to pass subsidiary norms through decrees. See also Suksi 2005, p. 246, where, in addition to this delegation issue, the issue of Ålandic regulation in the area of constitutional rights is pointed out as an area that relatively frequently creates problems in competence control.

[17]According to Koskelo 2009, p. 11 f., these infringements are very rare, but because such new legal institutions are continuously created that were not foreseen during the drafting of the 1991 Self-Government Act, the Supreme Court has the task to determine whether the new area is comparable in nature to the competencies of either the Legislative Assembly or the Parliament of Finland. See also Suksi 2005, p. 242 f., where reference is made to the issues of the Ålandic EU referendum and gene technology.

[18]According to Koskelo 2009, p. 12, Finland as a Member State is in breach of its international obligations if an Ålandic law conflicts with mandatory EU legislation. Because legislative power on issues relating to Finland's relations with foreign powers belongs to the Parliament of Finland, the Supreme Court has argued that the Legislative Assembly does not have the authority to pass laws that would place Finland in breach of a treaty, that is, in breach of its obligations as a Member State of the EU. For interpretations of the Supreme Court in this regard, see also Suksi 2005, pp. 264–271.

[19]Since an amendment of 2004 to the Self-Government Act, it is possible under section 20(3) of the Self-Government Act to pass into law and to promulgate such acts of Åland without submitting them to the competence control of the President that are related to the budget of the Åland Islands and that cannot be left pending during the four month period of presidential competence control. In

exercised the veto powers in relation to only 1–3% of Ålandic enactments per year, limitation of the competences of Åland is at a modest level. At the same time, the Legislative Assembly is politically active and interested in pushing the boundaries of its own competences. Therefore, at least some of the instances in which the veto has been used are likely to have been test cases designed to some extent intentionally by the Legislative Assembly with the purpose of claiming new legislative "territory". When the veto is recommended, the Supreme Court also formulates an opinion on whether the provisions that remain in the Ålandic enactment, that is, those which have not been found to be beyond competence, can enter into force.[20]

While the Supreme Court is in the driver's seat concerning competence control of Ålandic enactments before they are promulgated as acts of Åland, under Section 18 of the Self-Government Act, the situation is very different—and at the same time normatively confusing—concerning enactments of the Parliament of Finland. According to Section 74 of the Constitution of Finland, the Constitutional Committee of the Parliament is the authoritative organ for abstract constitutional review *ante legem* of draft laws (to some extent in a manner similar to the advisory opinions the Supreme Court of Canada gives in its references concerning draft acts). While this normally functions surprisingly well, in spite of the fact that the Constitutional Committee is composed of regular MPs, including the one representing voters in the Åland Islands, the constitutional review may also touch upon the issue of whether the Parliament is within its competence as concerns the jurisdiction of Åland on the basis of section 27 of the Self-Government Act. This competence control is mainly carried out in respect of international treaties that Finland has entered into and that may or may not have to be consented to by the Legislative Assembly of the Åland Islands. However, from time to time, ordinary enactments are also dealt with by Parliament that may raise questions about constitutionality in relation to the Self-Government Act. A case in point was the enactment of the Lotteries Act in 2001, where the Constitutional Committee formulated an amendment to the draft that it considered could be passed by the Parliament as an ordinary law. After being passed, the enactment was submitted to

---

such cases where there are particular reasons for the introduction of an act of Åland, the Government of the Åland Islands may decide that the act of Åland shall enter into force already before the President has had an opportunity to use her veto powers. If the President decides to use either the total or partial veto in relation to such an act that has been brought into force, the Government of the Åland Islands, the Government of the Åland Islands is under the duty to publish a declaration that the act or a part thereof ceases to apply from the day the declaration is published in the Statutes of Åland. This amendment to the Self-Government Act provoked serious criticism, because it could lead to legal uncertainty if a budget law were later repealed by the President. However, this possibility relating to budget laws has so far been used very sparingly and in a limited manner, mainly as a technical tool for adjusting levels of social allowances from the beginning of the budget year. The mechanism means that the Government of the Åland Islands declares, under an authorization of the Legislative Assembly based on particular reasons that the act of Åland enacted by the Legislative Assembly is such that it shall enter into force before the regular competence control has been undertaken.

[20]Koskelo 2009, p. 12.

the President of Finland, who used her powers to seek an opinion from the Supreme Court. After the Supreme Court had established that the enactment encroached onto the legislative competence of the Åland Islands,[21] the President returned the enactment to Parliament for reconsideration. The Parliament re-enacted the Lotteries Act with the same contents as before, thereby overriding the position of the President, but enacted at the same time an amendment to the Lotteries Act that entered into force at the same time as the Act itself and that erased the competence problem.[22]

The constitutional convulsions resulting from the amendment of the Lotteries Act revealed the bipolarity of the competence review as concerns the competence line between the Legislative Assembly and the Parliament and juxtaposed the Supreme Court and the Constitutional Committee as the supervisors of each of the two enumerations. It is highly unusual from the normative point of view that different provisions of one act have different interpreters and that situations could arise where the two interpreters express positions that are contradictory to each other. The inherent asymmetry of any autonomy arrangement is elevated to an entirely new level in Finland through the asymmetry related to the interpretation of the two enumerations of legislative powers where neither of the main actors is identified as the stronger one. The general principle of coherence in the legal order would, however, seem to require that one of the interpreters be recognized as having the upper hand, and in that respect it would probably have to be the Supreme Court in relation to both enumerations of legislative powers, rather than the Constitutional Committee, because the Parliament of Finland as a political body should not be recognized as having a superior position in relation to its counterpart in the Åland Islands, the Legislative Assembly. In spite of the confusing arrangement in terms of the control of the two legislative competencies, the system has functioned surprisingly well,[23] and it is exceptional for the Parliament of Finland to interpret its powers in the territory of the Åland Islands in a manner that encroaches onto the legislative powers of the Legislative Assembly.

---

[21]See Koskelo 2009, p. 16, for a cautious comment on the case 2001:79 of the Supreme Court.

[22]However, in the Supreme Court case 2005:27, the Court had to return to the topic to consider whether criminal liability could arise for marketing in the Finnish language over the internet of the games of the Åland Islands Slot Machine Association, with the gaming license granted on the basis of Åland legislation for the Åland Islands, so that persons living in mainland Finland could participate in the gaming. The Supreme Court was of the opinion that these lotteries had also been arranged in mainland Finland, where another gaming license, granted on the basis of legislation of the Parliament of Finland, is applicable. For that reason, the managing director, the director of marketing and the chairperson of the board of the Åland Islands Slot Machine Association were found criminally liable for a violation of the Lotteries Act. See also Suksi 2005, pp. 402–404.

[23]See also Jääskinen 2003, whose report arrives at the conclusion that it is not necessary to create any separate court instance of an independent nature to deal with the competence conflicts. See also Koskelo 2009, p. 17, for a comment on the questioning of the position of the Supreme Court after 80 successful years, concluding that there does not appear to exist any strong support for a modification of the system.

From time to time, courts of law need to determine whether, in a concrete case before them, they should follow a provision enacted by the Parliament of Finland or a provision enacted by the Legislative Assembly of the Åland Islands. In such situations of choice of law, the validity of an act in force in relation to either of the competence lists is not at issue, but rather which law should apply in a specific case. The judicial resolution in such a situation does not turn on whether the legislative decisions are outside the competence of the Legislative Assembly, because the competence issue has been tested already when the law was enacted, at least in so far as the legislation of the Åland Islands is concerned. This was made clear by the Supreme Court in the case 2018:16, which concluded that the contents of an Ålandic act cannot, after the act has been cleared by the competence control, be challenged on the ground that it violates the distribution of competence between the Parliament of Finland and the Legislative Assembly of the Åland Islands (although challenges under Section 106 of the Constitution on the basis of clear and evident contradiction with the Constitution could be presented; see below).[24] Instead, a court of law may, in relatively rare instances, have to choose, under the principles of Sections 18 and 27 of the Self-Government Act, whether to follow the Ålandic act or the act of the Parliament of Finland.[25]

Finally, there is the possibility that the application of a provision an Act of the Legislative Assembly of the Åland Islands is found to be in clear contradiction with the Constitution of Finland in the manner contemplated by Section 106 of the

[24]Supreme Court of Finland, case 2018:16, para. 10.

[25]See, e.g., the Supreme Court case 2005:87, where a person travelling as a customer on a vessel in the Åland Islands had exercised violence towards guards who had the task to maintain public order and security. The Supreme Court held that the incident as a whole clearly had a weaker link to merchant shipping in Section 27(13) of the Self-Government Act than to public order and safety under Section 18(6) in the Self-Government Act. The legislation in effect within this area of law in the territory of Åland, which belongs to the legislative competence of the Åland Islands under Section 18(6), was applied. See also the case of the Administrative Court of the Åland Islands of 15 November 2017, No. 80/2017, where the question was whether such provisions on conveyance tax were applicable also in the Åland Islands that had been included in an act of the Parliament of Finland the main purpose of which is to regulate matters for which the Legislative Assembly holds the legislative competence on the basis of the Self-Government Act. For municipalities, the Municipalities Act of mainland Finland had created a duty for municipalities to re-organize certain municipal utilities as companies in order to fulfil requirements in European Union competition law. Such corporations were also exempted from the conveyance tax. No such duty for municipalities existed in the Åland Islands, where the Legislative Assembly had not undertaken legislative measures, but a municipality had nevertheless incorporated its harbour functions in 2014, *inter alia*, with the aim of meeting the requirements of EU competition law. Because the tax provisions with the exemption were not territorially limited to mainland Finland only and because an exclusion of the incorporated harbour in the Åland would have resulted in higher tax for the harbour and thus constituted unequal treatment, the Administrative Court overturned the decision of the tax authorities whereby the application of the company of more lenient taxation had been denied. It was thus not held necessary that the Legislative Assembly should have had exercised its legislative competence with respect to municipal law in the same manner as the Parliament of Finland.

Constitution. While it is not entirely clear how this provision should function in relation to Ålandic acts with a view to the fact that the Self-Government Act creates a system of its own for prior competence control, it has been maintained that this provision is also available, although it has so far only been used once in relation to Ålandic acts when they are applied by courts of civil and criminal jurisdiction or by administrative courts (and only a few times since the year 2000 in relation to acts of the Finnish Parliament).[26] It appears, though, that this mechanism is not relevant for competence control in the conventional meaning of the term, in particular because competence problems in concrete situations are not very frequent.[27]

4.1.3 Denmark: Unilateral but Inactive Competence Control

In the Faroe Islands, the primary system of competence control established in the 1948 Home Rule Act is in principle unilateral, meaning that only the enactments of the Legislative Assembly of the Faroe Islands could be subjected to competence

---

[26]See the case of the Turku Court of Appeals of 10 January 2017 (R16/1828), where a driving prohibition for driving under influence of alcohol of 1 year 4 months, decided by the First Instance Court of the Åland Islands on the basis of the Ålandic Act on Driving Permit, was considered disproportionate and unacceptable, because in mainland Finland, the same offence would, under similar circumstances, have warranted a driving prohibition of 2–3 months (although the maximum time of prohibition in mainland Finland is much longer than the sentence in the Åland Islands). The Court of Appeals held that the discrepancy violates the equality provision in Section 6(1) of the Constitution of Finland and that the minimum provision in the Ålandic Act concerning the length of the driving prohibition should not be applied by reference to Section 106 of the Constitution. The judgment makes reference to the *travaux preparatoires* of the 1991 Self-Government Act, according to which the law in the Åland Islands and in mainland Finland should not deviate too much from each other. In its case 2018:16, the Supreme Court overturned the decision of the Court of Appeals and stated that it was within Ålandic legislative competence to establish a stricter scale of driving prohibition and that the application of the rule was not in evident contradiction with the Constitution in the meaning of Section 106 of the Constitution. This is a logical outcome, because in its Opinion of 23 December 2015, the Supreme Court held that the Legislative Assembly was not *ultra vires* when determining the contents of the criminalization for driving under influence, except that the low end of the scale (0.2 promille in the Åland Islands v. 0.5 in the rest of Finland) was a deviation from the general principles of criminal law, which are part of the legislative competence of the Parliament of Finland. Also, the main point with the autonomy arrangement is to make possible differences in legal rules of the Åland Islands and mainland Finland, depending on the political judgment of the Legislative Assembly of the Åland Islands, for instance, concerning the length of the driving prohibition.

[27]In addition to situations where legislative competence is tried, Section 60(2) of the Self-Government Act creates a mechanism for adjudication of administrative competence claims. If a dispute arises about the competence of a public authority of mainland Finland or the Åland Islands to take an administrative measure, authorities of the Åland Islands or of mainland Finland can present an application to the Supreme Court for the resolution of the matter. Such applications are relatively rare (see Supreme Court cases 1993:90, 1998:8, 2001:38, 2017:47 and 2017:48).

control through an adjudication committee.[28] Such unilateralism is by no means unusual in autonomy contexts and is practiced, for instance, in relation to the legislative competences of the Scottish Parliament. In the Faroe Islands, the adjudication committee system is based on Section 6(2) of the 1948 Home Rule Act. According to that provision, in case of doubt as to the competence of the Faroese Home Rule government in relation to the state authorities, the point at issue shall be referred to a committee consisting of two members appointed by the Danish Government and two appointed by the Government of the Faroe Islands together with three members of the Supreme Court of Justice appointed by its president, one of whom is appointed chairperson. Hence the adjudication takes place before a quasi- or semi-judicial body but, at least in principle, the political branch and the judicial branch of the committee are separated in the actual process. In case of agreement between the four members appointed by the Danish Government and the Faroese Government, the matter shall be held to be definitively decided, otherwise the matter shall be decided by the three judges from the Supreme Court of Denmark. The hope is thus that there will be a political settlement as to the competence claims, but if that is not forthcoming, there shall be a judicial settlement. According to Section 6(3) of the 1948 Home Rule Act, the Prime Minister can suspend a decision which has been referred to the committee until the committee has decided the matter.[29]

Two circumstances are of interest in this context. Firstly, the competence control created for Faroese legislation displays unilateralism in that according to Section 6 (2), it is only the Faroese legislative competences that can be controlled, not the part which the Danish Parliament controls.[30] Although this is somewhat similar to the situation in Finland with the Åland Delegation and the Supreme Court, there is in Finland the additional possibility of the Constitutional Committee of Parliament approaching the competence line from the perspective of the legislative powers of the Parliament of Finland so as to make the Finnish system at least slightly asymmetrical instead of unilateral. Secondly, and highly interestingly, the Faroese adjudication committee mechanism has apparently never been used, which seems to indicate that possible disputes between the authorities of Denmark proper and those of the Faroe Islands have been resolved informally or by means of negotiations

[28]From the Faroese side, the argument has been made that the adjudication committee could also try whether an act of the Danish Parliament is beyond competence. However, the wording of Section 6(2) is very clearly making the point of unilateral competence control by the adjudication committee.

[29]Rasmussen 2002, pp. 380–381. As pointed out by Rasmussen, the correct procedure for the Prime Minister would be to issue a Decree with Section 6(3) of the Home Rule Act as the legal basis and publish it in the Legislative Gazette of Denmark and in the Official Gazette of the Faroe Islands with the contents that a particular act of the Legislative Assembly or a part thereof is suspended until the decision of the adjudication committee exists.

[30]Rasmussen 2002, pp. 381–382. However, the point has been made on the part of a Faroese commentator that the committee could also inquire into whether national law is within the competence of the Parliament, a position that seems to contradict the wording of he provision. See speech by Eidesgaard 2006.

before the need to activate the dispute settlement mechanism has arisen.[31] In such situations, the home rule authorities may have voluntarily concurred with the conclusion that the competence line has been overstepped.[32] Another possibility is that disputes over competence conflict have been left unresolved.[33]

One consequence following from non-use of the mechanism may be that dispute resolution has been turned over to the courts of law, which can pass verdicts in trials of concrete issues on the question of which law, that of the Danish Parliament or that of the Legislative Assembly of the Faroe Islands, should be applied. It appears, however, as if very few judgments exist where the distribution of legislative powers has been an issue at all, which is rather surprising.[34] Only some indirect conclusions are possible on the basis of court cases.[35] If competence control through courts did

---

[31]As pointed out by Rasmussen 2002, p. 380, in the first instance, it is a political forum, the Legislative Assembly of the Faroe Islands, which interprets how the provisions in the Home Rule Act should be understood. Therefore, a number of potential disputes have been prevented from arising by means of self-control in the Legislative Assembly. See also speech by Jóannes Eidesgaard, 'Færøernes forfatningsmæssige stilling', at Nordic Lawyers' Academy on 24 August 2006 in Tórshavn, the Faroe Islands (on file with author).

[32]Rasmussen 2002, p. 381.

[33]á Rógvi 2013, p. 273.

[34]á Rógvi 2013, pp. 273–277, mentions five cases with greater or lesser relevance for the issue of distribution of legislative competence. See Rasmussen 2002, p. 383, who confirms that judicial praxis is rare. However, he makes reference to a case where a Danish Court of Appeals (Østre Landsrets 5. afdelings dom 15. juni 2001 [B0021006-SMH]: *Elsa Birgitta Petersen m.fl. v/ mandatar Føroya Lærarafelag imod Føroya Landsstýri*) found that legislation of the Faroe Islands on capping pay-rise for teachers of the Faroe Islands displayed a natural context with the competence field, education, which the Faroe Islands have. It was also taken into account that Danish authorities had not protested the fact that the Legislative Assembly enacted the law capping pay-rise. See also *Føroya Landsstýri mod Karsten Werner Larsen*, Ø.L.D., Østre Landsrets dom 5. juli 1983 i anke 5-295/1982, which is a case concerning the application of Faroese tax legislation. According to the case, the person working as a medical doctor in the Faroe Islandswas not originally an inhabitant of the Faroe Islands, but had taken up residence there. The tax authorities of the Faroe Islands decided on the basis of a provision from 1881 creating an exception for Faroese law that the more generous Faroese tax law would be applied only to those who during their childhood had acquired an established and natural link to the Faroe Islands, whereby regular Danish law would be applied to the MD. The Court of Appeals, however, ruled in favour of the MD, because the tax decision had set aside Section 10, Sub-section 2, para. 2, of the 1948 Home Rule Act when it puts the person in a less favourable situation than other inhabitants of the Faroe Islands for the reason that he had not earlier on been a Faroe Islander. The provision says that "no difference shall be made between Faroese and other subjects of the Danish state in legislation or administration". The Court found that the grounds presented by the tax office for denying lenient taxation were illegal, but the law itself was not, which means that an illegal (discriminatory) praxis had developed at the tax authority. This means that the Court did not have to enter into a direct discussion of constitutionality or competence. For a comment, see Myntti 1998, p. 275.

[35]See, e.g., *Almanna- og Heilsumálaráðið Landssjúkrahúsið mod A*, Ø.L.D., 13. september 2007 (5. afd., nr. B-574-07), where the Eastern Court of Appeals concluded that a patient who was resident in the Faroe Islands was entitled to compensation from the health authorities of the Faroe Islands for expenses due to treatment in Denmark proper, because the treatment that could be given in the Faroe Islands had proven ineffective and the patient had to seek treatment in Denmark proper. Similarly in *Færøernes Landsstyrelse og Heilsumálaráðið mod Region Hovedstaden*,

take place, it might display some symmetrical characteristics, provided that the courts of law considered themselves competent to try the legislative decisions of the Danish Parliament (which is not self-evident in this context; the Danish courts would normally not actively pursue the path of constitutional review). It seems to be sufficiently clear now, compared with the first decades of the home rule arrangement, that the enactments of the Legislative Assembly of the Faroe Islands are laws proper, not decisions of an administrative nature that could be subject to judicial review under Section 63 of the Constitution of Denmark.[36]

A question in this context is how the existence of a separate mechanism of competence adjudication in Section 6(2) of the Home Rule Act might affect the use of courts in the determination of competence. In that regard, it has been proposed that the existence of a particular mechanism for competence adjudication could preclude the raising of competence issues in court in a situation where the adjudication committee has made a decision on the same matter.[37] Moreover, the Court of First Instance in the Faroe Islands has ventured even farther, to the point of finding that the mere existence of the mechanism of competence adjudication in Section 6(2) is sufficient to preclude legal action that raises competence issues. In a case from 2016, the First Instance Court was of the opinion that the distribution of competence is based on negotiations and agreements between representatives of the Faroe Islands and Denmark (see Sect. 3.3). Therefore, the logic of the Home Rule Act and the Takeover Act is such that interpretation of the agreements and

Supreme Court of Denmark, 3. juni 2016 (1. afd., sag 160/2015), where it was found the authorities of Faroe Islands should pay to the region of Copenhagen for mental treatment of a person of Philippine nationality who had committed different crimes, including attempted murder, on a vessel registered in the Faroe Islands and was convicted by the court in the Faroe Islands, which is a state court, to care in a psychiatric institution on the basis of the Faroese law of procedure. The Supreme Court was of the opinion that the first instance court had a basis in the Faroese procedural law to decide that the person would be treated in a hospital in Denmark proper, without there existing any reference to the relevant provisions in the Faroese act concerning hospitals. The two cases indicate that if a practical issue arises in the Faroe Islands within the competence of the Faroe Islands, then the consequences of the decisions are the ultimate financial responsibility of the Faroe Islands also in situations where authorities in Denmark proper are used for the delivery of services. In the *travaus preparatoires* to the 2005 Takeover Act, situations of this kind are termed “interprovincial law”, aiming at determining whether rules that are in force for the Faroe Islands or rules that are in force for Denmark should be applied in a concrete case. In addition, interprovincial law would contain issues of mutual recognition of decisions by authorities of the Faroe Islands and Denmark, respectively. See Forslag til Lov om de færøske myndigheders overtagelse af sager og sagsområder, fremsat den 11. maj 2005 af statsministeren (Anders Fogh Rasmussen), section 6.4. It is estimated in this government proposal that the issues falling under the concept of interprovincial law will increase in the future.

[36]See, e.g., the case handed down by the Court of First Instance of the Faroe Islands, *Henrik Weihe Joensen mod Fiskimálaráðið*, Sorinskrivarin I Føroyum, 2. maj 2016 (sag nr. BS 899/2015), where reference to Section 63 is made by saying that the provision deals with review of the limits of the powers of public authorities, not of law-makers. Thus Section 63 is not perceived as a relevant provision for challenging the legislative enactments of the Legislative Assembly of the Faroe Islands.

[37]See Rasmussen 2002, p. 382.

resolution of issues concerning doubts about competence are for the parties to the agreements.[38] Provided that this is the general attitude of the Danish courts of law to competence claims in concrete court cases, it is only natural that the few court cases touching upon competence issues deal merely indirectly with distribution of powers. Lacking court praxis, it is somewhat difficult to say exactly where the competence line is drawn, although because it is easy to move the competence line by decisions of the Legislative Assembly of the Faroe Islands (see Sect. 3.3), it may generally be less important to know the exact location of the competence line at any given time.[39] However, in some rare situations the boundaries of competence may have great significance, as is shown by the debate on competence in the area of the established church, taken over by the Faroe Islands in 2007, in relation to the Danish Marriage Act (see Sect. 4.2.3).[40] In any event, it appears that the non-use of the existing adjudication mechanism and the unwillingness of the courts to try competence claims in concrete cases by implication places the resolution of competence issues entirely in the hands of the two governments, making such resolution predominantly a political matter prior to legislative action.

In addition, the position of the Faroe Islands in relation to Danish competence involves a practice of disallowance, albeit an inverted one. Since the latter part of the 19th century, legislation enacted by the Danish Parliament has contained statements as to whether or not the enactment applies to the Faroe Islands. However, even when a national act could apply to the Faroe Islands, it does not do so unless the Legislative Assembly is heard concerning the enactment, as established in Section 7 of the 1948 Home Rule Act, and unless it is brought into force

---

[38]See the case handed down by the Court of First Instance of the Faroe Islands, *Henrik Weihe Joensen mod Fiskimálaráðið*, Sorinskrivarin I Føroyum, 2. maj 2016 (sag nr. BS 899/2015). The case has not been appealed. The claimant presented the court with the issue of whether a Faroese Act on hunting the pilot whale (Løgtingslóg nr. 56 frá 19. mai 2015 um grind og annan smáhval, sum broytt við løgtingslóg nr. 44 frá 6. mai 2016), enacted within a legislative competence which had been with the Faroe Islands from 1948, could contain provisions on, *inter alia*, short detention of persons trying to prevent the whale hunt and confiscation of equipment that could be used to prevent the whale hunt, that were part of the Danish legislative competence under List B, para. 2: the police. However, the claim was dismissed by the Court because it did not arise for the claimant in a concrete legal dispute.

[39]It seems as if contradictions between Danish legislation and Faroese legislation could be resolved by relying on the ordinary principles of legal interpretation of *lex posterior* and *lex specialis*. See, e.g., Preliminary answers to questions raised by the Guernsey Constitutional Investigation Committee, Prime Minister's Office, Faroe Islands, 28 October 2014, para. 12 (on file with author). This would seem to indicate that in practical litigation of cases, the two legislative powers can concur and that the conflicts are resolved by means of the two principles of choice of law. As a consequence, the choice could fall on national law if it is later law or more specific law, or vice versa. If this indeed were the situation, the two jurisdictions would not actually be exclusive in relation to each other, but instead concurrent.

[40]See Rasmussen 2017, p. 60. As pointed out by Rasmussen, the legislative competence of established church belongs to List B of the Home Rule Act and to the list in the Takeover Act that requires negotiations. This means that the matter can be taken over only after negotiations between the authorities of the Faroe Islands and Denmark. According to Rasmussen, the negotiations determine if and to what extent competence can be taken over.

by means of a proclamation in the Official Gazette of the Faroe Islands. This actually places the entering into force of Danish national law in the Faroe Islands in the hands of the Legislative Assembly of the Faroe Islands and gives it a possibility to disallow national law. This sub-state disallowance over national law has been practiced quite extensively and has produced a situation where it often takes quite a long time for even the initiation of a royal proclamation in the Faroe Islands on the entering into force of a national act. As a consequence, parts of the legal order of the Faroe Islands consist of very old national law enacted before 1948, because the entering into force of later national law has not been dealt with in the Legislative Assembly.[41] With legislative powers increasingly in the hands of the Legislative Assembly of the Faroe Islands, it is possible that, for instance, old provisions in Danish criminal law, long since amended or repealed in Denmark but still in force in the Faroe Islands, may now be modernized by the Legislative Assembly.

4.1.4 Concluding Remarks

Taken together, the three countries analysed here range from symmetrical competence control (Canada) to asymmetrical competence control (Finland) and further to unilateral competence control (Denmark; which, however, has never been utilized, although the mechanism exists in the 1948 Home Rule Act). In relation to the enactments of the Legislative Assembly of the Åland Islands, competence control is active and systematic, because it will in principle take place in relation to each piece of Ålandic legislation in at least the Åland Delegation, although not all legislation is analysed by the Supreme Court of Finland *ex ante*, only those pieces of law identified as problematic by the Åland Delegation. In addition, there is the possibility of budget-related legislation to be analysed *ex post*.

In Canada, competence control is passive and unsystematic *ex post* in the sense that the law is enacted by either the federal or the provincial legislature (save for so-called reference cases, which are *ex ante* procedures concerning draft laws), but may be declared to be outside of the legislator's competence in individual cases when disputes arise, which is mainly in actual practice, that is, when the law is applied. Competence control in relation to the laws of the Faroe Islands displays features which are difficult to characterize in terms of active/passive or systematic/unsystematic competence control, because practice is completely lacking. However, it appears that the system in Denmark is mainly passive and unsystematic, as the initiative has to be taken separately for each Faroese act that needs to be reviewed (which so far has never happened) and not all enactments are controlled.

[41] See, e.g., speech by Jóannes Eidesgaard, 'Færøernes forfatningsmæssige stilling'. at Nordic Lawyers' Academy on 24 August 2006 in Tórshavn, the Faroe Islands (on file with author), and speech by Ísfeld 2013.

4.2 Methods of Managing the Distribution of Competence

4.2.1 Canada and the Provinces: Interpretations to Enhance Cooperative Federalism

The idea communicated in the legal order of the three countries is that it is possible to establish two law-makers each of which have exclusive competences enumerated in lists of matters, however constructed. This is the starting point for divided sovereignty in these countries. Very often, real life (including political life) is not organized according to the two categories of enumerations so that it falls neatly into either the list of matters for the national parliament or the list of matters for the sub-state entity.[42] Realities of all sorts, including the evolution of society and law, may require the existence of complementary or supplementary methods, some officially instituted in the constitutional framework governing the relationship between the country and the sub-state entity and some born of the practical necessity of coordination for the management of various issues.[43]

The interpretations of the Canadian courts have during the past century developed the relationship between the federation and the provinces from an understanding of watertight compartments between the two enumerations towards cooperative federalism.[44] Indeed, in situations where a province has legislated in an

---

[42]This is true for Canada, for instance, in the uncertainties over legislative competence concerning the so-called Métis population, originally a mix of aboriginal Indian population and French-speaking Europeans. Although the Métis are since 1982 mentioned in Section 35 of the Constitution as an indigenous people of Canada, it has not been clear whether the legislative competence concerning the Métis is on the federation or on the provinces, because Section 91(24) only makes reference to Indians, although the Métis have existed at least from mid-17th century. Therefore, the federation has legislative competence only as concerns Indians, while the Métis population has, in many ways, fallen between the two legislative competences, although the two legislative orders have enacted law for them, while at the same time denying that they actually have the legislative competence. In the case of *Daniels v. Canada (Indian Affairs and Northern Development)*, [2016] 1 SCR 99, 2016 SCC 12 (CanLII), the Supreme Court held that Métis and non-status Indians are "Indians" under Section 91(24), which means that the determination of their legal position is a matter of the federal law-maker.

[43]For a general and thorough commentary on all aspects of federalism and distribution of powers in the Canadian Constitution, see chapters 5, and 15–33 in Hogg 2014. See also Inwood 2013, p. 107 f., and Smith 2010, pp. 110, 112–119.

[44]See Hogg 2014, s. 5.8: "The essence of cooperative federalism is a network of relationships between the executives of the central and regional governments." Hogg 2014, s. 5.8: "At any given time, there are over 150 organizations, conferences and committees involved in intergovernmental liaison, indicating the vast array of consultative organisms within the Canadian federation. In addition, of course, there are countless informal contacts among civil servants of all governments." See also Brouillet 2011, pp. 615–618. However, the principle of cooperative federalism could not, in the case of *Quebec (Attorney General) v. Canada (Attorney General)*, [2015] S.C.J. No. 15, 2015 SCC 14 (S.C.C.), prevent the Parliament from enacting under Section 91(27) on "criminal law" such federal legislation, originally enacted under the same heading, that mandated the destruction of data concerning the possession of firearms license instead of giving that data to the

area where the federal law-maker is also competent to legislate and has passed legislation, a paramountcy of federal law in relation to provincial law has been developed by means of court interpretation, with the construction that "provincial law is not rendered invalid or *ultra vires*; nor is it repealed; it is rendered 'inoperative'".[45] This paramountcy doctrine, which, as mentioned above, is not found in explicit provisions of the Constitution, is of a unilateral nature and usually has the effect of limiting provincial legislative powers.[46] It has developed from an initial "watertight compartments doctrine"[47] upheld until the 1930s through a covering-the-field-doctrine,[48] meaning resolution of inconsistency "between federal and provincial laws based on an imputation that federal law 'covers the field' or carries a 'negative implication' forbidding supplementary provincial law in the same field", and further via an express contradiction position[49] into a more teleological assessment of whether "federal law has a purpose that would be frustrated by a provincial law".[50]

It appears as if the main issues were how exclusive the exclusive powers actually are and how the two fields of exclusive powers can be made to co-exist parallel to each other in a modern society, established in a three-step analytical framework elaborated by the Supreme Court of Canada (see below). Much of the doctrine was in place by the mid-1980s, but towards the end of the 2000s and in the 2010s, a number of important federalism cases were resolved that at least in part redefined the equilibrium between the federation and the provinces. It is not possible to deal with the entire body of case-law developed by the Supreme Court here and do justice to all the doctrinal facets, only to bring out some main characteristics.

---

provinces to facilitate the creation by provincial law of provincial licensing regimes for firearms. See generally Inwood 2013, pp. 79 f., 218–225.

[45]Hogg 2006, p. 335. In that sense, rendering a piece of law inoperative is similar to the application of Section 106 of the Constitution of Finland.

[46]Ryder 2006, pp. 347 f.

[47]There is, however, some element of a watertight compartments thinking in the case *Consolidated Fastfrate inc. v. Western Canada Council of Teamsters* [2009] S.C.J. No. 53, [2009] 3 S.C.R. 407 (S.C.C.), in which provincial legislation's validity was upheld on the basis of Section 92(13) on "property and civil rights" against federal law in an exception to provincial legislative power established in Section 92(10)(a) on "other works and undertakings", because the decision of the majority (6–3) drew on the textual and historical interpretation of the relevant division of powers provisions. In the case of *Tessier Ltée v. Quebec (Commission de la santé et de la sécurité du travail)*, [2012] S.C.J. No. 23, 2012 SCC 23 (S.C.C.), the stevedoring activities of a company operating in a province constituted a minor part of its business operation and the company was therefore, on the basis of Section 92(10 and 13) considered to be under provincial legislation for reasons of "local works and undertakings" and "property and civil rights in the province" and not to come under federal power in Section 91(10) of "navigation and shipping". No "pith and substance" test was explicitly used in the case.

[48]Hogg 2014, s. 16.4(a).

[49]The concept of "operational conflict" was used in *British Columbia v. Lafarge* [2007] S.C. J. No. 23, 2007 SCC 23.

[50]Hogg 2006, pp. 336–342. For an account of the evolution of the doctrine, see paras. 53–62 in *Reference re Securities Act*, [2011] S.C.J. No. 66, 2011 SCC 66, [2011] 3 S.C.R. 837 (S.C.C.).

The analytical framework applied to a piece of law, whether federal or provincial, when inconsistency with the distribution of legislative powers in Sections 91 and 92 is claimed, has three steps: the pith and substance test, the interjurisdictional immunity test and the paramountcy test, executed in this order.[51] Although the three-step method of cooperative federalism provides flexibility for the interpretation and application of the constitutional doctrines concerning distribution of legislative powers, "it can neither override nor modify the division of powers itself. It cannot be seen as imposing limits on the valid exercise of legislative authority."[52]

The competence analysis starts with a so-called "pith and substance" test. It tries to extract the dominant feature, the main thrust or the true nature and character of the law, after which the court assigns the legislation to a federal or a provincial head of power. The intention is to detect whether the impugned legislation aims at a subject matter outside the jurisdiction of the legislative body enacting it.[53] The aim of this test is explicitly not to enforce exclusivity; as stated in *Rogers Communications Inc. v. Châteauguay (City)*, "[w]hen conducting a pith and substance analysis, a court must avoid adopting the watertight compartments approach, which this Court has in fact rejected".[54] This is so because the pith and substance test instead creates tolerance for the co-existence of laws of the two orders of government in the same field, that is, recognizes the possibility of overlap *intra vires* between federal and provincial laws as long as the enactment of the one legislator does not enter the essence of law-making powers of the other legislator.[55] However, if such an intrusion into the essential character of the powers of the other law-maker is found, there is a successful validity attack at hand and the review will

---

[51]*Rogers Communications Inc. v. Châteauguay (City)*, [2016] 1 SCR 467, 2016 SCC 23 (CanLII), para. 35, although the interjurisdictional immunity test is relatively limited (para. 61), which means that the second step can often be passed.

[52]*Rogers Communications Inc. v. Châteauguay (City)*, para. 39.

[53]Hogg 2014, from s. 15.4 until s. 15.5(a); Wright 2010, pp. 640–641.

[54]*Rogers Communications Inc. v. Châteauguay (City)*, para. 37.

[55]As the Supreme Court said in the *Reference re Securities Act*, [2011] S.C.J. No. 66, 2011 SCC 66, [2011] 3 S.C.R. 837 (S.C.C.), "the Canadian constitutional law has long recognized that the same subject or 'matter' may possess both federal and provincial aspects. This means that a federal law may govern a matter from one perspective and a provincial law from another. The federal law pursues an objective that in pith and substance falls within Parliament's jurisdiction, while the provincial law pursues a different objective that falls within provincial jurisdiction (*Canadian Western Bank*, at para. 30). This concept, known as the double aspect doctrine, allows for the *concurrent application* of both federal and provincial legislation, but it does not create *concurrent jurisdiction* over a matter (in the way, for example, s. 95 of the Constitution Act, 1867 does for agriculture and immigration)." However, in the case of *Rogers Communications Inc. v. Châteauguay (City)*, paras. 50–52, where the Court did not agree that there would exist a double aspect within the radiocommunications area in such a way that both orders of government could legislate within that area, because the area was already within federal powers, not within provincial powers.

result in the legislation in question being declared of no force or effect, that is, the impugned law will be found invalid (*ultra vires*).[56]

In *Rogers Communications Inc. v. Châteauguay (City)*, the City of Châteauguay exercised its powers based on provincial legislation *intra vires* within Section 92 (13) and (16) to prevent a license holder in telecommunications area from constructing a radiocommunication antenna system on a piece of property within the city for a period of 2 plus 2 years. However, since 1932 the federal legislator has exclusive competence in the area of telecommunications on the basis of Sections 91 (29) and 92(10)(a), including the power to choose the location of radiocommunication infrastructure.[57] The Supreme Court concluded that the pith and substance of the measure of the City "is not the protection of the health and well-being of residents or the development of the territory but, rather, the choice of the location of the radiocommunication infrastructure" and found that the measure of the City was "*ultra vires*, because it constitutes an exercise of the power over radiocommunication, which is an exclusive federal power".[58] Invalidity is ex tunc in a case where *ultra vires* is found, that is, from the moment of entering into force of the

[56]In the *Reference re Securities Act*, *ibidem*, the Supreme Court found that the pith and substance of the draft Act was outside of the federal power in Section 91(2), "the regulation of trade and commerce" and entered the provincial legislative powers established in Section 92(13, 16) on "property and civil rights" and on "matters of a merely local or private nature", namely the regulation of contracts, property and professions. In *Canadian Western Bank v. Alberta*, [2007] S.C.J. No. 22, 2007 SCC 22, application of provincial insurance legislation under section 92(13) to banks created under section 91(15) by federal legislation was found constitutionally valid in the "pith and substance" test, without any need to engage interjurisdictional immunity or paramountcy. In *Chatterjee v. Ontario (Attorney General)*, [2009] S.C.J. No. 19, [2009] 1 S.C.R. 624 (S.C.C.), provisions in a provincial criminal remedies act were considered valid on the basis of Section 92(13) concerning "property and civil rights" because they only had incidental impact on the federal criminal powers in Section 91(27). In *Quebec (Attorney General) v. Lacombe*, 2010 SCC 38, [2010] 2 S.C.R. 453, the Supreme Court (7-1-1) held that a zoning by-law enacted within section 92(13, 16) on "property and civil rights" and "matters of a merely local or private nature in the province" intruded with its pith and substance into the area of aeronautics created on the basis of the chapeau of Section 91 power "to make laws for the peace, order, and good government of Canada", that is, its national concern branch, so as to become invalid. In *Reference re Assisted Human Reproduction Act*, 2010 SCC 61, [2010] 3 S.C.R. 457, a very divided court ruling (4-4-1) ended up with upholding the constitutionality of typical criminalizations in a federal act under Section 91(27) on federal criminal powers, but found unconstitutionality with respect to regulatory and administrative parts of the federal act for reasons of excess of the same Section 91(27) and of intruding into provincial legislative powers of 92(7, 13, 16) concerning the "establishment, maintenance and management of hospitals", "property and civil rights in the province" and "matters of a merely local or private nature in the province". To the extent of division of powers matters, *Canada (Attorney General) v. PHS Community Services Society*, [2011] S.C.J. No. 44, [2011] 3 S.C.R. 134 (S.C.C.) established that the federal Controlled Drugs and Substances Act was *intra vires* of the federal parliament, because in pith and substance, the act contained valid exercises of the federal criminal law power under Section 91(27). Even if the provisions of the act had the incidental effect of regulating provincial health institutions, it did not mean that they are constitutionally invalid.

[57]*Rogers Communications Inc. v. Châteauguay (City)*, para. 42.

[58]*Rogers Communications Inc. v. Châteauguay (City)*, paras. 46, 53.

enactment.[59] If only a part of a law is challenged, the provision of the act may be saved under the so-called ancillary doctrine or necessary incidental doctrine, but that requires that the statute considered as a whole must be valid.[60] It is also possible to use this test in relation to draft laws in situations where they are referred to the Court for an advisory opinion. This doctrine of "pith and substance" facilitates the cohabitation of two legislators, but the "pith and substance" test is possibly somewhat tilted in favour of the validity of federal law over provincial law.

The second part of the analytical framework is the "interjurisdictional immunity" test, which asks whether law, having been found to be constitutionally valid, is inapplicable to particular persons, places or things by virtue of those subjects being within the exclusive jurisdiction of the other level of government.[61] In practice, interjurisdictional immunity provides for a limited degree of immunity mainly for federal undertakings from laws enacted by the provinces and thus deals with the application of the law. After the *Canadian Western Bank* and *Lafarge* judgments, the scope of this doctrine is narrower than it used to be, because it is not enough that the impugned law affects undertakings regulated by the other order of law, it must actually impair their activities.[62] As clarified in *Rogers Communications Inc. v.*

---

[59]Brun et al. 2008, p. 195 f. For a radical example, see *Re Manitoba Language Rights*, [1985] 1 SCR 721, 1985 CanLII 33 (SCC), where the Supreme Court declared the unilingual Acts of the Legislature of Manitoba to be invalid and of no force and effect from 1890 on, but ordered them to be temporarily valid until such time that a new determination could be made determination of the minimum period necessary for translation, re-enactment, printing and publishing of the Acts of the Manitoba Legislature in English and French.

[60]See Hogg 2014, s. 15.6, 15.9(c). For the ancillary powers test, see *General Motors of Canada v. City National Leasing*, [1989] S.C.J. No. 28. As pointed out in Wright 2010, pp. 640–641: "The court is first required to determine whether the provision encroaches on the jurisdiction of the other level of government. If not, the provision is *intra vires* the enacting legislature. But if so, the provision may nonetheless still be *intra vires* the enacting legislature if: (a) it is a part of a valid legislative scheme; and (b) it is sufficiently integrated in to that legislative scheme. The final step turns on the seriousness of the encroachment: where the encroachment is minimal, it is sufficient if the provision is 'functionally related' to the legislative scheme; but where the encroachment is not minimal, the provision must be 'truly necessary' or 'integral' to the legislative scheme. As pointed out by Elliott 2008, p. 478, "the 'double aspect' doctrine tolerates the legislation of one order of government having 'incidental effects' on the jurisdiction of the other". As pointed out in Brouillet 2011, pp. 622–623, the application of the ancillary powers doctrine could be seen as favouring the federal parliament's powers, but from the case of *Lacombe*, "it is now clear that it can also be applied for the benefit of the provinces. In *Lacombe*, however, the Supreme Court decided that the conditions for its application had not been met."

[61]See Hogg 2014, s. 15.8(c), 15.9; Furey 2007, p. 597 ff.; Hogg and Godil 2007, p. 623 ff. See also *Bell Canada v. Quebec,* [1988].1. S.C.R. 749.

[62]*Quebec (Attorney General) v. Canadian Owners and Pilots Association*, 2010 SCC 39, [2010] 2 S.C.R. 536, in which a divided court (7-2) found that provincial law on protection of agricultural land that had the effect of preventing aerodromes, enacted under Section 92(13, 16) of "property and civil rights" and "matters of a merely local or private nature" as well as Section 95 on "agriculture" and thus valid, violated the federal general power in the area of aeronautics enacted on the basis of the chapeau of Section 91 "to make laws for the peace, order, and good government

Châteauguay (City), a case where the Supreme Court decided not to apply the doctrine of interjurisdictional immunity, although the doctrine was considered, the corporation holding a federal telecommunications license was obliged under federal law to implement the license according to its specifications. Therefore, it is possible to conclude that the telecommunications corporation became in that capacity an entity exercising precedence-based federal power on the basis of Section 91(29) and 92(10)(a), that is, a federal undertaking.

In addition, the use of interjurisdictional immunity is limited by the requirement that it should generally be applied in situations already covered by precedent, and therefore, "absence of prior case law favouring its application to the subject matter at hand will generally justify a court proceeding directly to the consideration of federal paramountcy".[63] A successful applicability attack results in the legislation being left intact as drafted, but the law is "read down" so as to be inapplicable in the context in question. This test has mainly been used to protect federal acts, rarely provincial acts, in a manner which produces some lack of reciprocity, but this doctrine was limited by the Supreme Court in a number of relatively recent cases.[64]

The third part of the analytical framework is the "paramountcy" doctrine, that is, whether a provincial law, found to be both valid and applicable, is inconsistent with valid federal law and therefore inoperative under the doctrine of paramountcy. The doctrine of paramountcy can be viewed as an exception to the "pith and substance" doctrine, because it provides for the priority of federal law in cases where there is, in individual application situations, a direct conflict between federal and provincial law that affects the operability of provincial law.[65] In the case of *Canadian Western Bank*, the Supreme Court summarized the doctrine by holding that conflict can manifest itself in two ways, in narrow impossibility of dual compliance when it is not possible to comply with both laws at the same time, and in broader frustration of

---

of Canada". The paramountcy doctrine did not apply, because there was not found any operational conflict or frustration of federal purpose. In *Canada (Attorney General) v. PHS Community Services Society*, [2011] S.C.J. No. 44, [2011] 3 S.C.R. 134 (S.C.C.), it was concluded that the doctrine of interjurisdictional immunity does not apply. "Decisions about what treatment may be offered in provincial health facilities do not constitute a protected core of the provincial power over health care and are not, therefore, immune from federal interference. In addition, the doctrine of interjurisdictional immunity is narrow, and its premise of fixed watertight cores is in tension with the evolution of Canadian constitutional interpretation towards the more flexible concepts of double aspect and cooperative federalism. To apply it here would disturb settled competencies and introduce uncertainties for new ones."

[63]Canadian Western Bank, paras. 77, 78.

[64]As concluded in Hogg 2014, s. 15.8(f), "[t]he doctrine of interjurisdictional immunity ought to be reciprocal, protecting provincial subjects from incursions by *federal* laws", with examples provided. See also the cases of *Reference re Assisted Human Reproduction Act* and *Canada (Attorney General) v. PHS Community Services Society* for arguments that interjurisdictional immunity should also apply to provinces, not only to the federation.

[65]As concluded in the case of *Marine Services International Ltd v. Ryan Estate*, [2013] S.C. J. No. 44, 2013 SCC 44 (S.C.C.) "federal paramountcy applies where there is an inconsistency between a valid federal legislative enactment and a valid provincial legislative enactment, but not between a common law rule and a valid provincial law".

federal purpose when the operation of a provincial law would frustrate the purpose of federal law.[66] However, the "standard for invalidating provincial legislation on the basis of frustration of federal purpose is high".[67] A successful operability attack results in provincial legislation being declared inoperative for as long as the conflict in question continues to exist.[68] In areas where the paramountcy doctrine can be applied, the federal Parliament is therefore ultimately supreme and the provincial legislatures are subordinate.[69]

As can be noticed on the basis of the above account of the steps of review, paramountcy is, in many ways, a last instance after the pith and substance test and the interjurisdictional immunity test (in the limited space this latter test can be used). In that capacity, paramountcy is relatively narrowly drawn in a manner that does not support any general supremacy doctrine or federal preemption in Canada. At the same time, the Supreme Court of Canada has showed considerable judicial restraint since the mid-1980s in comparison with earlier decades in invalidating either the federation's or a province's legislation for reasons of incursion into the other law-maker's sphere of competence.[70] When it has expressed itself on matters,

---

[66] *Canadian Western Bank v. Alberta*, [2007] S.C.J. No. 22, 2007 SCC 22. For an analysis of the paramountcy doctrine, rich in case materials, see Hogg 2014, Chap. 16. See also Wright 2010, p. 649.

[67] *Marine Services International Ltd v. Ryan Estate*, [2013] S.C.J. No. 44, 2013 SCC 44 (S.C.C.).

[68] As stated in Hogg 2014, s. 16.6, the paramountcy doctrine "will affect the operation of the provincial law only so long as the inconsistent federal law is in force. If the federal law is repealed, the provincial law will automatically 'revive' (come back into operation) without any reenactment by the provincial Legislature".

[69] See *British Columbia v. Lafarge* [2007] S.C.J. No. 23, 2007 SCC 23, in which the Supreme Court did not find the interjurisdictional immunity test applicable, but decided the case on grounds of federal paramountcy, because there was the federal Marine Act enacted on the basis of section 91(10) and a provincial land use by-law enacted on the basis of section 92(8, 13, 16) simultaneously in force, both incapable of simultaneous enforcement so as to create an operational conflict because a judge could not have given effect to both the federal law and the municipal law, and therefore, federal law set aside provincial law. In the case of *Quebec (Attorney General) v. Canada (Human Resources and Social Development* [2011] S.C.J. No. 60, [2011] 3 S.C.R. 635 (S. C.C.), no operational conflict was found, but instead a frustration of federal purpose. The Court held that the purpose of the challenged measure, created under Section 91(2A), is to ensure the integrity of the employment insurance system by making it possible to recover amounts owed, including benefit overpayments, in a simple and summary fashion, without regard for the provincial rules respecting exemption from seizure. "This purpose would be frustrated if the Commission were to comply with the provincial provision creating an exemption from seizure." Therefore, provincial law was inoperative owing to a conflict of legislative purposes. However, in the case of *Marine Services International Ltd v. Ryan Estate*, [2013] S.C.J. No. 44, 2013 SCC 44 (S.C.C.), it was found that a provincial act, apparently enacted under Section 92(13) on "property and civil rights", which establishes a no fault regime to compensate for workplace-related injury, "does not frustrate the purpose of section 6(2) of the federal Marine Liability Act, which was enacted under Section 91(10) to expand the range of claimants who could start an action in maritime negligence law. The provincial act simply provides for a different regime for compensation that is distinct and separate from tort."

[70] See, e.g., Hogg 2014, s. 16.3(a).

it has, by regarding the Constitution as a living tree, opted for a dynamic interpretation of the federal heads of competences, that is, agreed to enlargement of the federal legislative competence in relation to the legislative competence of the provinces so as to produce "unintended" areas of concurrent powers where federal paramountcy might rule, but where there also is space for inter-governmental agreements.[71] Against this background, it has been maintained that "it is increasingly important for provincial laws to be aligned with federal legislative policies if they are to operate in areas of overlapping jurisdiction. This is not good news for provincial autonomy."[72]

However, as mentioned in the *Reference re Securities Act* case, para. 90, the Supreme Court does not engage itself in an inquiry into what would be the best resolution in terms of policy: "Efficaciousness is not a relevant consideration in a division of powers analysis. Similarly, references in past cases to promoting fair and effective commerce should be understood as referring to constitutional powers that, because they are essential in the national interest, transcend provincial interests and are truly national in importance and scope. Canada must identify a federal aspect distinct from that on which the provincial legislation is grounded. The courts do not have the power to declare legislation constitutional simply because they conclude that it may be the best option from the point of view of policy. The test is not which jurisdiction—federal or provincial—is thought to be best placed to legislate regarding the matter in question. The inquiry into constitutional powers under ss. 91 and 92 of the Constitution Act, 1867 focuses on legislative competence, not policy."

In contrast to dynamic interpretation of federal powers, the Supreme Court has upheld provincial legislative enactments on the basis of less dynamic forms of interpretation: "The Court has simply interpreted well-established principles in a manner that has been favourable to provincial legislative jurisdiction. In particular, the Court has used the pith and substance doctrine and its corollary, the incidental effects doctrine, to uphold provincial statutes so long as they have had a strong connection to a matter within provincial jurisdiction. The fact that these statutes also had substantial impact on matters outside of jurisdiction was characterized as incidental, irrelevant for the purposes of constitutional validity."[73] Thus, federal law has also been set aside when in conflict with provincial powers established in

---

[71] Ryder 2006, at 354–356. On inter-governmental agreements, see also Cameron and Simeon 2002, pp. 49–71. Inter-governmental agreements are generally not enforceable through court action, but include instead other dispute resolution mechanisms, like a committee or a panel system, which is the case in the Agreement on Internal Trade, Consolidated Version (2015), at http://www.ait-aci.ca/wp-content/uploads/2015/08/ait_en.pdf (accessed on 9 November 2015), although the general philosophy is that they are not meant to be broken "within family". In case a party to such an agreement would experience a problem on the part of another party, it would normally be reasonably easy to terminate such an agreement, but the operation of such agreements usually do not produce conflicts, because the aim of them is to ensure a smooth administration of some issue. See also Culat 1992, p. 617, and Inwood 2013, p. 256.

[72] Ryder 2006, at 372.

[73] Ryder 2006, at 362. See also Inwood 2013, p. 111 f.

Section 92 of the Constitution. The divisions within the Supreme Court of Canada on federalism issues that became apparent through case law from approximately 2007 until 2013 seem to have the effect of "equalizing" at least to some extent the position of the provinces under Section 92 with that of the federation under Section 91. As maintained by the Supreme Court in the *Securities Act Reference* case, "notwithstanding the Court's promotion of cooperative and flexible federalism, the constitutional boundaries that underlie the division of powers must be respected. The 'dominant tide' of flexible federalism, however strong its pull may be, cannot sweep designated powers out to sea, nor erode the constitutional balance inherent in the Canadian federal state".[74] This is so because the Canadian federation "rests on the organizing principle that the orders of government are coordinate and not subordinate one to the other. As a consequence, a federal head of power cannot be given a scope that would eviscerate a provincial legislative competence."[75]

The evolution of the doctrine of concurrent application of legislative powers in Canada seems to have resulted in a situation where co-habitation of similar federal and provincial rules is possible and where their effect on a person is interpreted so as to try to uphold the validity of both, as far as this is possible. If not, under the paramountcy doctrine, the provincial law is rendered inoperative in the particular situation to the extent of the inconsistency which frustrates the purpose of federal law (that is, the direct contradiction between the federal and provincial law), but the provincial law is not revoked in part or *in toto*. The ethos of the Canadian federal system therefore seems to be based on a respect by the courts of the popularly elected law-maker, whether of the federation or a province. However, at the same time, the Supreme Court facilitates the operation of the federal principle by promoting cooperative federalism, which leads to expectations of cooperation between the federal level and the provincial level in working out the necessary regulatory schemes.

Thus the exclusive nature of the two lists of legislative powers in Sections 91 and 92 of the Canadian Constitution is not at all as exclusive as one might think, but during the decade after 2006, the interpretation of the two spheres of legislative competence appears to have found a new equilibrium that takes the provinces into consideration in a better way than previously: "the need to respect the principle of exclusivity embodied in the text of Sections 91 and 92, at least insofar as the core

---

[74] *Reference re Securities Act*, [2011] S.C.J. No. 66, 2011 SCC 66, [2011] 3 S.C.R. 837 (S.C.C.), para. 62. In para. 134 of this advisory opinion, the Supreme Court ruled that the federal "Securities Act as presently drafted is not valid under the general branch of the federal power to regulate trade and commerce under s. 91(2) of the Constitution Act, 1867", which means that the trade and commerce power of the federation was capped and the legislative competence of the provinces was recognized, mainly within property and civil rights under section 92(13), with implications also for provincial legislative jurisdiction over matters of a merely local or private nature in section 92(16), namely the regulation of contracts, property and professions. In its ruling, the Court held that "the proposed Act overreaches genuine national concerns".

[75] *Reference re Securities Act*, para. 71.

areas of each head of power are concerned" is a compelling one,[76] but in practical governance not quite as dominant as one might expect on the basis of the court cases. One feature of the Canadian system is that the federal law-maker and the provincial law-maker may, in some situations, legislate in identical terms on some issue, such as highway traffic offences or the stock exchange, each within its competence, and that this is possible from a constitutional point of view under the double aspect doctrine,[77] without activating federal paramountcy for reasons of, for instance, federal law covering the field so as to set aside the operation of the provincial law.[78]

In Canada, due to inter-governmental cooperation, there is actually a lot more asymmetry than the two lists of enumeration in the Constitution indicate, in particular in the areas of education, administration of tax collection[79] and pensions plans, and immigration. For instance, immigration, which is one of the four concurrent jurisdictions (as distinguished from areas of concurrent application), is in part regulated by means of agreements which the federation concludes separately with each province.[80] The current agreement concerning Quebec dates back to

[76]Elliott 2008, at 497–498. See also Leclair 2010, pp. 567, and 574: "Parliament's enumerated powers are, for the most part, 'electorally unattractive'. Interprovincial transportation, communications and national defence might have had some appeal in 1867, but with the advent of the welfare state, health, social welfare and education have become the politicians' preferred fields of battle. The sorrowful nature—if I may be allowed this expression—of the central government's enumerated heads of power explains the enthusiastic recourse to the spending power witnessed during the 1960s through the 1980s and beyond. However, in view of the spending power's dubious constitutionality in the eyes of many, the central government has tried, quite legitimately, to find ways of expanding its existing legislative powers." and at 574: "In a sense, the division of powers is an 'all or nothing' game. A level of government either has a power to regulate (directly through one of its exclusive heads of jurisdiction or indirectly by way of its ancillary power) or it does not. Once recognized, the exercise of such a power cannot be modulated according to the wishes of the courts."

[77]Hogg 2014, s. 15.5(c), 15.9(b), from 16.5(a) (b). As stated in Hogg 2014, s. 16.5(a), "[t]here is no reason why duplication should be a case of inconsistency once the negative implication or covering the field test is rejected. On the contrary, duplication is 'the ultimate in harmony'. The argument that it is untidy, wasteful and confusing to have two laws when only one is needed reflects a value which in a federal system often has to be subordinated to that of provincial autonomy. Nor does the latter value disappear when provincial law merely duplicates federal law, because the suspension of a provincial law may create a gap in a provincial scheme of regulation which would have to be filled by federal law—a situation as productive of untidiness, waste and confusion as duplication."

[78]Hogg 2014, s. 16.3(a), from 16.4(a).

[79]See Hogg 2014, s. 6.4.

[80]For the inter-governmental agreements on immigration, see http://www.cic.gc.ca/english/department/laws-policy/agreements/index.asp (accessed on 9 November 2015). See also Inwood 2013, p. 113 f., who estimates that there would exist more than 1500 inter-governmental agreements, of which around 85% are bilateral agreements.

1991, and according to this, Quebec can for demographic reasons select immigrants arriving in Quebec.[81] This inter-governmental cooperation is also a feature of Canadian federalism which the Supreme Court of Canada is willing to support when resolving cases where private claimants attempt to overthrow legislative decisions: if the outcome of legislation is endorsed by the two orders of government by means of an agreement, the Court is likely to favour a resolution of the case that is in accord with the inter-governmental harmony rather than one which sides with the private claimant.

In addition, the Canadian federal government from time to time uses its financial resources to achieve policy goals that are not foreseen in the enumerations distributing legislative powers between the federation and the provinces but that could fall into the legislative competence of the provinces. This has often occurred so that "federal intervention has secured nation-wide plans of health, education and welfare—matters within provincial jurisdiction".[82] These may take the shape of federally-initiated shared-cost programmes that tempt the provinces into participating by means of financial rewards, sometimes of a conditional nature (although the conditionality dimension seems to have been diminishing).[83] Taken together, these programmes, which lie outside of federal legislative authority, have "amounted to a heavy federal presence in matters which are within provincial legislative responsibility".[84] It should be noted that in addition, Section 36 of the Constitution Act, 1982 establishes a scheme for equalization payments by which the federation supports those provinces which have fewer resources.[85]

---

[81]See Canada–Québec Accord relating to Immigration and Temporary Admission of Aliens of 5 February 1991, at http://www.cic.gc.ca/english/department/laws-policy/agreements/quebec/can-que.asp (accessed on 9 November 2015). The agreement means that Canada establishes the total number of immigrants that the country can admit and admits immigrants up to a portion the Quebec has determined (and which is equal to the share of Quebec's population of the total population of Canada) and who meet Québec's selection criteria unless they are inadmissible, and upon their arrival, Québec provides reception and integration services, reasonably compensated for this by Canada. Québec also undertakes to receive a percentage of refugees and persons in similar situation at least equal to the percentage of immigrants it accepts. See 'The Canada-Québec Accord Made Easy-Federal-Provincial Relations' by Renée Joyal on November 2, 1994, at http://www.cic.gc.ca/english/department/laws-policy/agreements/quebec/can-que-guide.asp (accessed on 9 November 2015).

[82]Hogg 2014, s. 5.8.

[83]Hogg 2014, s. 6.7. See also Inwood 2013, pp. 114 f., 190–209.

[84]Hogg 2014, s. 6.8(a). See also the case of *Re Canada Assistance Plan*, [1991] 2 S.C.R. 525, where the Supreme Court affirmed broad federal powers "to authorize grants to the provinces for use in fields of provincial jurisdiction and the power to impose conditions on the recipient provinces", as commented in Hogg 2014, s. 6.8(a).

[85]Hogg 2014, s. 6.6, Inwood 2013, pp. 197–200, 204 f.

4.2.2 *Finland and the Åland Islands: Watertight Compartments with Some Modifications*

Although far-reaching exclusivity, close to upholding an idea of "watertight compartments" of an earlier Canadian type, exists between the legislative competences of the Parliament of Finland and the Åland Islands,[86] some pith and substance and even ancillary powers thinking is from time to time visible in the opinions of the Supreme Court concerning the competence of the Åland Islands.[87] In addition, an element of interjurisdictional immunity is present in the relationship between an enactment of the Legislative Assembly of the Åland Islands and the Parliament of Finland in that it is generally not permitted for the Legislative Assembly to try to regulate matters in such a manner that authorities of the State or the tasks of State authorities are affected by Ålandic provisions. This might be thought relatively self-evident on the basis of the Self-Government Act and on the basis of the principle that administrative competence follows from legislative competence, but the Supreme Court has dealt with a number of cases of this sort.[88]

A pith and substance argumentation was used, for instance, in an Opinion from 2003 concerning amendments to an Ålandic Act on Tobacco, which had the aim of implementing on behalf of Finland, in the Åland Islands, EC directive 2001/37/EC of the European Parliament and of the Council of 5 June 2001 on the approximation of the laws, regulations and administrative provisions of the Member States concerning the manufacture, presentation and sale of tobacco products (the so-called Tobacco Directive). The enactment of the Legislative Assembly contained, *inter alia*, a provision about the sale of snuff intended for oral use. The Supreme Court concluded in its Opinion that the rules in the Ålandic law are, with respect to legislative competence, mainly to be allocated to the area of health in Section 18 (12) of the Self-Government Act and business activities in Section 18(22), and that the competence in the area of criminal law according to Section 18(25) was also relevant. In addition, the enactment contained provisions about consumer

[86]See, e.g., Opinions of the Supreme Court of 12 September 2017 (Dnr OH2017/136; lowering of voting age in Ålandic Local Government Act from 18 years to 16 years was violation of the competence of the Parliament according to Section 27(1) (constitutional law), because Section 14 (3) of the Constitution sets the voting age at 18 years in municipal elections); Opinion of 12 September 2017 (Dnr OH2017/135; three sections of the Ålandic Act on municipal rescue services were contrary to the constitutional right of municipalities to self-government in Section 121 of the Constitution); Opinion of 3 March 2017 (OH2017/8; the Legislative Assembly of the Åland Islands did not have the competence to include in an Ålandic Act a provision which aimed at setting aside a provision that had had been enacted within the area of the legislative competence of the Parliament of Finland).

[87]For a relatively early example, see the Opinion of the Supreme Court of 19 June 1979, that is, during the operation of the 1951 Self-Government Act. However, there may well exist earlier cases of a similar nature.

[88]See, e.g., Opinion of the Supreme Court of 28 August 1998 (Nr. 2743) on the Ålandic Act on Security of Leisure Boats (with an EU law dimension), Opinion of 22 June 2000 (Nr. 1339) on the Police Act of Åland.

protection, which according to Section 27(10) is a competence of the Parliament of Finland. The conclusion of the Supreme Court was that because the provisions in the main dealt with the protection of health of the users of tobacco products, the competence to pass rules was with the Legislative Assembly of the Åland Islands.[89] Such pith and substance argumentation is not uncommon in the Opinions of the Supreme Court.

Similarly, thinking along the lines of pith and substance or the leading feature of the legislation under evaluation is present in a case concerning public procurement. The interpretation of the competence line concerning whether public procurement is administrative procedure within Ålandic competence or competition law within the competence of the Parliament of Finland was first raised in an Opinion from 1994,[90] in which public procurement was deemed to be entirely within the competence of the Åland Islands. In 2007, when the Legislative Assembly passed new legislation on this matter, a majority of the Supreme Court held that the dimension of competition law in the legislation had evolved such that the legislation was now to a great extent within the legislative competence of the Parliament of Finland on the basis of Section 27(10) of the Self-Government Act.[91] The reason may have been that EU law on public procurement was increasingly emphasizing the competition aspect, which would imply that the leading features of public procurement law were increasingly situated in the area of competition law. The President nevertheless sided with the minority of the Supreme Court, which thought the legislation was still chiefly about administrative procedure and as such within Ålandic competence on the basis of Section 18(1 and 4). As a consequence, the Ålandic law was not vetoed, but could enter into force.

In 2017, further legislation in the area of public procurement was passed by the Legislative Assembly, but this time the Supreme Court held that the legislation was within Ålandic competence. However, the Court reiterated its "dictum" from the Opinion of 2007 that it may become necessary to re-evaluate a competence issue. The Court concluded that although the regulation of public procurement had evolved further during the preceding years, the dimensions of competition law had not changed so significantly that there was reason to re-consider legislative competence. As a consequence, the Supreme Court was of the opinion that previous praxis, including the decision of the President, did not give reason to re-consider legislative competence in this case and that the previous line of interpretation would be followed under the present circumstances.

The above Opinion appears, however, to open up the possibility of reconsideration of the competence line in these matters so that legislative competence could shift to the Parliament of Finland, should public procurement law, in particular that of the EU, evolve further into the area of competition law and away from

[89]Opinion of the Supreme Court, 18 August 2003 (nr 1958).

[90]See Opinion of the Supreme Court, 12 September 2017 (Dnr OH2017/134).

[91]Opinion of the Supreme Court, 2 July 2007 (Dnr OH2007/75).

administrative procedure. Such a development would upset the traditional view about the fields of competences. It should not be so that an interpretation of what the focus of EU law is has an impact on which side of the competence that public procurement is placed, Åland for public authorities of Åland or Parliament for competition law. If it has an impact, then the EU law is a cause for competence leakage from Åland to Finland which is similar to the problems experienced on the basis of the 1920 Self-Government Act, when the exercise of treaty powers by the State of Finland determined that material legislation would be the competence of the Parliament, not of the Legislative Assembly of the Åland Islands.

In an Opinion concerning the Ålandic Act on the Amendment of the Ålandic Act on the Application in the Åland Islands of the Parliament's Enactments concerning Alcohol,[92] the Supreme Court noted that in early drafting documents for the Act it had been pointed out that the obligation on the holder of an alcohol license to offer a receipt when alcohol is sold belongs to the legislative competence of the Parliament of Finland, while the Ålandic Act itself covers the same issue within the Ålandic jurisdiction. For reasons such as the fight against corruption, tax control, accounting, and consumer protection, the proposal of the government of the Åland Islands to the Legislative Assembly suggested, on the basis of Section 27(42) and the principles underlying the Self-Government Act, that the law-making competence was with Parliament. However, the Supreme Court held that there was no reason to focus on small terminological differences and that handing over a bill, receipt or other certificate can be connected to the act of verifying that payment of a purchase of alcohol has taken place.

Neither the fact that the Parliament of Finland was going to receive a legislative proposal that would introduce an overlapping rule, nor the fact that both the Government of Finland and the Government of the Åland Islands were of the opinion that general rules on provision of receipts are within the legislative competence of the Parliament were relevant factors in the determination of whether the Åland Islands could have legislative competence in the matter. Instead, the Supreme Court held that if no general duty to provide a receipt existed, it was natural to derive such a duty from the area of law within which the duty had been introduced. Therefore, it was appropriate to assign the limited duty to hand over a receipt on the occasion of serving alcoholic beverages to the same area of law as the actual sale, which was within the competence of Åland. Thus, a business operator in the Åland Islands who has a license from the Government of Åland to serve alcoholic beverages can also be placed under a duty on the basis of the alcohol legislation of Åland to hand over a receipt. The fact that this duty serves several objectives of control does not diminish its proximity to the license to serve alcoholic beverages. It seems that in this case, the Supreme Court reasoned that the introduction of a duty to hand over a receipt, in the Ålandic Act on the sale of

[92]Opinion of the Supreme Court, 6 June 2013 (Dnr OH 2013/86).

alcoholic beverages, was an ancillary provision to Section 18(13) and therefore within the competence of the Legislative Assembly.[93]

In spite of the fact that the Ålandic and mainland Finnish legislative competences are exclusive in relation to each other, it is not prohibited for the Legislative Assembly to import provisions from Finnish law. Indeed, under section 19(3) of the Self-Government Act it is possible, for the purposes of achieving uniformity and clarity of an act of Åland, to include provisions within acts of Åland on matters falling under the legislative powers of the Parliament, provided that in their substance, they coincide with the corresponding provisions of an act of Parliament. The inclusion of such provisions in an act of Åland shall, however, not alter the separation of the legislative powers of the Legislative Assembly and the Parliament of Finland.

Such inclusion of provisions from laws enacted by the Parliament of Finland in the acts of Åland results in enactments of a mixed nature in the Åland Islands. This arises because the exercise of legislative powers in the Åland Islands does not always produce clear-cut regulation of legal relationships solely within the Ålandic sphere of competence, but sometimes steps over to the other side of the competence line. As a consequence, some of the provisions that must necessarily be included in the act of Åland to achieve regulatory logic might not belong to the legislative competence of the Legislative Assembly. Section 19(3) makes it possible to enact coherent and systematically structured acts of Åland by using, in an act of Åland, norms that belong to the legislative competence of the Parliament of Finland and that materially coincide with the corresponding norms in an act of the Parliament of Finland.[94] This possibility to enact mixed legislation aims to ensure that an act of Åland is informative in relation to all those persons to whom the act is applied. The incorporation of provisions from legislation enacted by the Parliament of Finland does not, however, change the legislative competence between the two lawmakers in any way. If a deviation from competence has taken place, then the Legislative Assembly has made an incursion into the legislative competence of the Parliament of Finland. A deviation in choice of words only does not constitute a breach of competence unless it also involves a material deviation from competence.

The consequence of Section 19(3) of the Self-Government Act is that an act of Åland can contain provisions that have originally been enacted within the

[93]A consequence of simultaneous application of the Ålandic Act and the draft act to be enacted by the Parliament of Finland, once adopted, would be that there would, in the Åland Islands, exist a double sanctions system (criminal law in the Åland Islands and administrative law sanctions according to the legislation enacted by the Parliament) for an act that only means that no receipt has been handed over in the process of selling and serving alcoholic beverages. The Supreme Court was of the opinion that this was not a circumstance that affected the distribution of legislative competence and that, if such a situation would occur, the rule of *ne bis in idem* would become applicable.

[94]In Scotland, a similar result may be produced through adjudication of the competence line by courts. In Scotland and the UK, courts of law may interpret the purpose of a Scottish act through the "pith and substance" test so that a Scottish act is considered to be within competence even when containing a provision that belongs to UK competence.

competence of the Parliament of Finland. In such a situation, the provision originally enacted by the Parliament of Finland continues to be applicable in the Åland Islands on the basis of the legislative competence of the Parliament of Finland.[95] The further consequences of this become apparent if the Parliament of Finland amends the original provision, because then the provision amended by the Parliament of Finland applies in the Åland Islands as amended, but the Ålandic mixed act would continue to feature the original wording in its unamended form. At such a point, the aim of producing an informative act of Åland is, of course, countered. In order to satisfy the need of an individual or a business enterprise to always receive correct information about the contents of legal provisions, acts of Åland of a mixed nature should be automatically amended if the Parliament of Finland amends provisions that have been incorporated into acts of Åland.

As concerns the extent to which an act of Åland can contain mixed provisions, it has sometimes been suggested that the proportion of provisions stemming from an act enacted by the Parliament of Finland should not exceed 50%. There is no such rule in the Self-Government Act, and the interpretations of the Supreme Court do not indicate that such a rule of proportion would be imposed in practice. However, there exist some opinions of the Supreme Court that indicate that Ålandic enactments that consist entirely or mainly of provisions that belong to the legislative competence of the Parliament of Finland cannot be passed by the Legislative Assembly.[96]

It is also important to note that the Legislative Assembly may, within its legislative competence, enact so-called acts of reference (Swedish: *blankettlag*), which means that an act enacted by the Parliament of Finland is made applicable in the Åland Islands within the legislative competence of Åland by means of an act of Åland. The situation is in this respect different from the acts of a mixed nature, because the acts of reference are enacted within the competence of Åland. This method of enactment is often used to legislate on technical standards, such as foodstuffs, product safety, chemicals and motor vehicles.[97] By choosing to enact an act of reference, the Legislative Assembly decides to apply the same provisions as

---

[95]See, e.g., Opinion of the Supreme Court of 2 June 2017 (Dnr OH2017/90; Section 1 of the Ålandic Act on Public Order contained a rule that is a part of general criminal law and as such, applicable national law in the Åland Islands, but the inclusion of the national rule in the Ålandic Act was not a violation of the competence of the Parliament of Finland); Opinion 31 March 2017 (Dnr OH2017/35; inclusion of some provisions on market control of certain products from an Act of Parliament did not violate the competence line);

[96]See, e.g., the following Opinion of the Supreme Court: 5 April 1963, 19 June 1979.

[97]See, e.g., Opinion of the Supreme Court of 3 March 2017 (OH2017/7; provisions within the legislative competence of the Parliament on consumer protection and standardization could be included in an Ålandic Act) and Opinion of 3 March 2017 (Dnr OH2017/6; similar issues concerning standardization and consumer protection). See also Silverström 2008, p. 45, who makes the point that the implementation of technical EU directives may cause the Legislative Assembly to choose such a legislative strategy that directives are implemented by way of referring to the relevant state implementing legislation. "However, there are also many directives requiring Ålandic legislation which are not simple copies of State legislation".

in mainland Finland, and in such a situation it is beneficial if the normative situation in the Åland Islands can follow the development of the provisions in mainland Finland. Typically, an act of Åland of this sort makes reference to the act or acts enacted by the Parliament of Finland by name and number and declares that any future amendments made by the Parliament of Finland to the act or acts will also apply in the Åland Islands.

The method of act of reference has also often been used in the implementation of EU law, because the short implementation period prescribed by an EU directive may leave insufficient time for the law-drafting mechanism of the Åland Islands to react. In such situations, the Government and the Legislative Assembly of the Åland Islands may choose to enact the act of Åland according to the wording used by the Parliament of Finland, which leads to certain savings in time and resources. The capacity to draft laws in the quantities required by changes in the formal legal environment (the EU, international treaties) and by changes in society is, naturally, limited in the Åland Islands.[98] Therefore, from time to time, acts of reference are used to incorporate by Ålandic legislative decision the contents of an act passed by the Parliament of Finland.

Sometimes, acts of reference are enacted by the Legislative Assembly so that they not only make reference to an act passed by the Parliament of Finland, but also contain one or some material provisions, such as an exception of some sort to the act of the Parliament of Finland. In such cases, the act of reference becomes an act of a mixed nature, too, albeit of a different kind than the above-mentioned acts. The use of acts of reference may thus from time to time lead to normative situations which are not easy to grasp for the individual or even the public authorities and courts that implement such acts.[99]

In Section 32 of the Self-Government Act, a particular normative procedure is established that should not normally affect the formal distribution of powers but that distributes administrative tasks between the Åland Islands and state authorities. The procedure uses so-called consent decrees, issued by the President of Finland after the Åland Delegation has given an opinion on the draft. The purpose of consent decrees is to make possible transfers of duties belonging to the state administration

---

[98]As pointed out in Silverström 2008, p. 45, only eight civil servants are responsible for the drafting of legislation in the Government of the Åland Islands, which is very little in comparison with any Member State, although the volume of EU norms relevant for the Åland Islands is almost at the same level as the volume of EU norms relevant for a Member State.

[99]One example of such a legislative technique could be the Act of Åland on the Application on the Åland Islands of some Acts on Re-Districting of Municipalities (SoÅ 76/1997). According to this Act of Åland, the Act on Re-Districting of Municipalities (SoF 1196/1997) of mainland Finland shall be applied in the Åland Islands, but with exceptions specified in the Act of Åland. The exceptions mentioned in the particular Act of Åland transfer those functions that in mainland Finland were held by the Ministry of the Interior, the provincial government and the Council of State to the Government of the Åland Islands. In addition, this Act of Åland prescribes that costs that are caused by the implementation of the legislation on the re-districting of municipalities in the Åland Islands are payable out of the means of the budget of the Åland Islands instead of being paid from the state budget.

to administrative agencies of the Åland Islands or duties of an agency of Åland to the state administration. Such transfer may be agreed upon by the Government of the Åland Islands and the Government of Finland, and the transfer may be arranged for a certain period of time or until further notice. If notice is given on an existing agreement by either of the two parties, the relevant consent decree shall be amended or repealed as soon as possible and in any case within one year from the date of the notice. Unless the decree is amended or repealed within the said time, the agreement shall be deemed to have been terminated one year after the notice. This means that it is the agreement between the two parties that controls the validity of the decree. The mechanism of consent decrees has, however, some normative implications for the legislative powers of the Legislative Assembly, because under sub-section 2 of the provision, an act of Åland which is contrary to a consent decree shall not apply to the extent of the contradiction while the decree is in force.[100] Here the principles of the hierarchy of norms are, at least to some extent, turned upside down, but in practice, the Åland Islands can always terminate an agreement concerning a consent decree that raises competence problems.

Consent decrees are prepared jointly by the executive organs of the Åland Islands and mainland Finland, and they typically deal with public services in areas that belong either to the legislative competence of the Legislative Assembly or the Parliament of Finland, which would otherwise be unavailable for some reason to the inhabitants of the Åland Islands. Examples of matters where consent decrees exist are the production, by the population registry authorities of the state of Finland, of the list of voters for elections of the Legislative Assembly and municipal boards in the Åland Islands, and the emergency transportation of persons for medical reasons on vessels belonging to the Coast Guard. In these cases, organs of the Finnish state administration have agreed to take care of functions which are formally the responsibility of the Åland Islands.[101] Hence there exists a certain measure of inter-governmental cooperation between the autonomy arrangement and the state, discernable also in several other respects in the 1991 Self-Government Act by means of references to consultation and cooperation between the Governments of Finland and the Åland Islands.[102] Although the competence line is strict, the practical management of issues requires cooperation.

---

[100]In this respect, the mechanism has a similar effect as interjurisdictional immunity in Canada.

[101]Decree on the Taking Care of some Tasks that Relate to Elections to the Legislative Assembly and to Municipal Elections as well as to Advisory Municipal Referendums in the Åland Islands (SoF 375/1999) and Decree of the President of the Republic concerning the Tasks of the Border Guards in the Åland Islands (SoF 420/2004).

[102]There is also the possibility under Section 48 of the Self-Government Act to give from the State budget extraordinary grants for particularly great non-recurring expenditures that may not justifiably be expected to be incorporated in the budget of Åland, provided that the purpose of the grant is within the competence of Åland; this mechanism is seldom used.

4.2.3 Denmark and the Faroe Islands: Political Determination Leading to Uncertainty over Competence

As explained above, the adjudication committee created under Section 6(2) of the 1948 Home Rule Act has never been called to resolve any dispute concerning competence. Therefore, it may be conjectured that this committee is not a body that actively performs any dispute resolution function and as a consequence there do not exist any interpretations which could enable characterisation of the dispute resolution in the way possible concerning Canada in relation to the provinces or Finland in relation to the Åland Islands. However, competence issues have arisen between the two entities, Denmark proper and the Faroe Islands, and these competence issues have been solved through political negotiations between the governmental bodies of Denmark and the Faroe Islands.[103] Given the ease with which the Faroe Islands can take over legislative competence from the Parliament of Denmark, one practical possibility from the Faroese side, at least after 2005, would be to transfer the contentious matter from the Parliament to the Legislative Assembly of the Faroe Islands according to the procedures of the 2005 Takeover Act, that is, either with or without negotiations.

One example of a complicated competence issue is the decision of the Legislative Assembly to bring into effect the Danish Marriage Act and legislation on the legal effect of related civil procedures in the Faroe Islands, but only after Section 14(2) of the Marriage Act has been revoked or modified so that it does not give the right to a same sex couple to have their civil marriage blessed by a priest in the established church.[104] The Faroe Islands have not taken over competence in relation to marriage, and the situation revealed different understandings about the location of legislative competence between Faroese authorities and Danish ministries and also between and within the Danish government ministries.

In particular, it is interesting that the *travaux preparatoires* to the Faroese legislation on the established church, a matter taken over in 2007, clearly conclude that marriage legislation continues to be in Danish hands and that marriage legislation has not been touched upon in negotiations between Faroese and Danish authorities, a conclusion that the Danish authorities have overlooked in their replies to the debate. The consequence of this appears to be, on the basis of an opinion of the Office of the Prime Minister of Denmark, that some implicit transfer of competence can take place in a manner that does not involve negotiations or require the participation of the Legislative Assembly of the Faroe Islands. Against this background, it has been stated that the interpretation of competence may have moved, at

[103]For examples, see Rasmussen 2002, pp. 378–382. Such a situation was at hand also in relation to the sub-soil resources, originally on List B over matters that could be transferred after negotiations. Negotiations between the governments of Denmark and Faroe Islands were carried out during a long period of time before the matter was taken over by the Faroe Islands in 1992.

[104]Rasmussen 2017, p. 60.

least in this case, from a formal delineation of competence in conjunction with transfer of competence to a more material delineation of competence.[105] Perhaps there is, in terms of the Canadian doctrine, a move from watertight compartments (formal delineation) towards some pith and substance thinking or ancillary effect of provisions established within the Faroese competence.

4.2.4 Concluding Remarks

It seems the interpretative praxis concerning the distribution of legislative powers is very developed in Canada, where this praxis has been in the making for 150 years through litigation, potentially in all courts, but peaking in the interpretations of the highest court instance, which was the Judicial Committee of the Privy Council until 1949 and thereafter the Supreme Court of Canada. Because the competence line between the Parliament of Finland and the Legislative Assembly has been revised several times during the past 100 years by means of adoption of new Self-Government Acts (and sometimes by amendments thereto), the short time before each subsequent version of the Self-Government Act has not created the same pressure to interpret the competence line through the opinions of the Supreme Court of Finland. Instead, the need to change the competence line has been met through adoption of new Self-Government Acts. At the same time, however, some interpretations along the lines of pith and substance are visible in the Opinions of the Supreme Court. As concerns the Faroe Islands, the absence of interpretations from the non-functional adjudication committee in combination with the apparent unwillingness of the courts to deal with competence issues in concrete cases, of course, changes the nature of the determination of the competence line, making it more political. In situations of doubt, the governments of Denmark and the Faroe Islands have negotiated and reached solutions on how the Home Rule Act should be understood.[106]

At the same time as there exist mechanisms and also practice for the resolution of competence issues, it seems perfectly clear that any distribution of legislative powers also needs other mechanisms for resolving or managing competence issues, namely political ones. The Faroe Islands stands out in this respect because of its reliance on negotiations of various kinds for the resolution of competence issues, as concerns the practical management of the competence line, for the transfer of law-making powers from the Danish Parliament, and also as a first step in the process before the adjudication committee (which has never been used). Also the Åland Islands arrangement is, in practice, premised on extensive contacts between the governmental authorities of Finland and the Åland Islands, explicitly referred to in several provisions of the 1991 Self-Government Act (in particular Section 30),

[105]Rasmussen 2017, pp. 62–64, 65.
[106]Rasmussen 2002, p. 381.

but also in the enumerations of law-making powers in Sections 18 and 27. Furthermore, inter-governmental cooperation and executive federalism has become a trade-mark of Canadian federalism,[107] promoted even by the Supreme Court of Canada by means of its expectation of co-operative federalism. In all jurisdictions dealt with here, the management of the competence line appears to have a relatively strong political side to it which supplements the enforcement of the legal competence line.

References

á Rógvi K (2013) West-Nordic constitutional judicial review. Djøf Publishing, Copenhagen

Brouillet E (2011) Canadian Federalism and the principle of subsidiarity: should we open the Pandora's box. Supreme Court Law Rev 54(2):601

Brun H, Tremblay G, Brouillet E (2008) *Droit constitutionnel*, 5thedn. Les Éditions Yvon blais Inc.

Cameron D, Simeon R (2002) Inter-governmental relations in Canada—the emergence of collaborative federalism. Publius 32(2):49

Culat D (1992) Coveting thy neighbour's beer: intergovernmental agreements dispute settlement and interprovincial trade barriers. Les Cahiers de Droit 33:617

Eidesgaard J (2006) 'Færøernes forfatningsmæssige stilling', speech at Nordic Lawyers' Academy on 24 August 2006 in Tórshavn, the Faroe Islands (on file with author)

Elliott R (2008) Interjurisdictional immunity after Canadian Western Bank and Lafarge Canada Inc.: the supreme court muddies the doctrinal waters—Again. Supreme Court Law Rev 43(2):433

Forslag til Lov om de færøske myndigheders overtagelse af sager og sagsområder, fremsat den 11. maj 2005 af statsministeren

Furey JG (2007) Interjurisdictional immunity: the pendulum has swung. Supreme Court Law Rev 42(2):597

Guernsey Constitutional Investigation Committee (2014) Prime Minister's Office, Faroe Islands, 28 October 2014 (on file with author)

Hogg PW (2006) Paramountcy and tobacco. Supreme Court Law Rev 36(2):335

Hogg PW (2014) Constitutional law of Canada, 5th edn supplemented, vols 1 and 2. Thomson & Carswell, Toronto [NB! References to Hogg 2014 are to sections in the supplemented loose-leaf volume, not to pages.]

Hogg PW, Godil R (2007) Narrowing interjurisdictional immunity. Supreme Court Law Rev 42(2):623

Inwood GJ (2013) Understanding Canadian federalism—an introduction to theory and practice. Pearson, Toronto

Ísfeld S (2013) Deputy Minister of Foreign Affairs of the Faroe Islands, speech of June 2013 (on file with author)

Jääskinen N (2003) EU:s behörighet och Åland. Utredningsman Niilo Jääskinens utredning. Statsrådets kanslis publikationsserie 7/2003. Statsrådets kansli, Helsingfors

Koskelo P (2009) The role of the Supreme Court of Finland in issues relating to the division of powers between the Finnish state and Åland'. In: Sia Spiliopoulou Åkermark (ed) Constitutions, autonomies and the EU. Åland Islands Peace Institute, Mariehamn

[107]See Inwood 2013, pp. 18, 64–80, 84 f., 91–101, 218–225, 257. See also Smith 2010, p. 155 f.

Leclair J (2010) Please, draw me a field of jurisdiction: regulating securities, securing federalism. Supreme Court Law Rev 51(2):555

Myntti K (1998) Minoriteters och urfolks politiska rättigheter. In: Juridica Lapponica 18. Lapplands universitet, Rovaniemi

Palmgren Sten (1995) Landskapet Ålands lagstiftning. Nordisk Administrativt Tidsskrift 1:22–32

Rasmussen S (2002) Til hjemmestyreloven os skiller. Ugeskrift for Retsvæsen, nr. 43, 26. oktober 2002, pp 377–383

Rasmussen TV (2017) Opportunistisk dansk fortolkning af det færøske hjemmestyrets lovgivningskompetence. Ugeskrift for Retsvæsen, nr 6, februar 2017, pp 60–65

Ryder B (2006) The end of umpire? Federalism and judicial restraint. Supreme Court Law Rev 36(2):345

Silverström S (2008) Implementation of EU legislation in the Åland Islands. In: Sia Spiliopoulou Åkermark (ed) Constitutions, autonomies and the EU. Åland Islands Peace Institute, Mariehamn

Smith DE (2010) Federalism and the constitution of Canada. University of Toronto Press, Toronto

Suksi M (2005) Ålands konstitution. Åbo Akademis förlag, Åbo

Wright WK (2010) Facilitating intergovernmental dialogue: judicial review of the division of powers in the Supreme Court of Canada. Supreme Court Law Rev 51:625

Chapter 5
Resolution of Competence Claims Concerning Legislative Matters not Mentioned in Enumerations

The above enumerations of legislative powers purport to be exhaustive, that is, to cover all conceivable legislative matters, or at least those conceived of at the time when the enumerations were first enacted. Over the course of time, new matters have been placed on the lists by way of constitutional amendment in Canada and Finland, and in Denmark a change was brought about through the 2005 Takeover Act, albeit in a very particular manner. However, a problem in this regard was apparent for the Åland Islands when the 1920 Self-Government Act was still in force: new legislative matter and matters resulting from treaties between Finland and other States were automatically channelled into the legislative competence of the Parliament of Finland. This problem was remedied in the 1951 Self-Government Act in a manner now evident in the two lists of enumerations in the 1991 Act. In Canada, provisions that could accommodate social, economic and technological developments were inserted in Sections 91 and 92 as early as 1867.

In the case of Canada, the federal Parliament has a constitutional basis for legislating on matters not defined in the federal enumeration in the so-called POGG powers established in the opening words of Section 91 "to make laws for the peace, order, and good government of Canada in relation to all matters not coming within the classes of subjects assigned exclusively to the Legislatures of the Provinces". This is often referred to as a federal residual or residuary power, but it is not of a general nature and remains rather limited.[1] The POGG power may be understood as being matched in Section 92(16) by a corresponding grant of rather open-ended legislative powers for the provinces concerning "generally all matters of a merely local or private nature in the province". "Thus, any matter which does not come within any of the specific classes of subjects will be provincial if it is merely local or private (s. 92(16)) and will be federal if it has a national dimension (s. 91, opening words)."[2]

[1]Hogg 2014, s. 17.1.
[2]Hogg 2014, s. 15.9(e). See also Inwood 2013, pp. 58, 109 f.

M. Suksi, *Double Enumeration of Legislative Powers in a Sub-State Context*, SpringerBriefs in Law, https://doi.org/10.1007/978-3-319-90921-9_5

The provinces are free to legislate within their enumerated heads of power in Section 92, for instance on the basis of Section 92(16), also on issues that might be considered new, that is, in relation to issues that did not exist at the time of the adoption of the Constitution Act, 1867, just as the federation may try to fit new legislative issues and phenomena within the existing heads of power of Section 91. The POGG power of the chapeau of Section 91 is to be used by the federation to fill legislative *lacunae* or respond to national concerns or emergencies.[3] However, the relevance of newness of an issue to the use of the POGG power has been denied.[4] Instead, the POGG power is circumscribed not only by the explicit provincial heads of power in Section 92, but also by the priority given to the application of the explicit federal heads of power in Section 91 before the POGG power is even engaged.[5] It has been held that the reason for the existence of residual powers in the chapeau of Section 91, which would seem to conform with the definition of a typical autonomy arrangement,[6] was the wish to create a stronger central government in Canada than existed in the United States at the time of the adoption of the Constitution Act, 1867: "Of course, there is no logical reason why this result should follow from the mere fact that the federal Parliament has the residue of power: the actual extent and importance of the residue depends by definition on the extent and importance of the provincial powers which are subtracted from the residue."[7]

The gap-filling power is not very extensive, because "[t]here are very few undoubted gaps in the scheme of distribution [of powers—MS] which have to be filled in this way".[8] The gap-filling power was established in a series of relatively early cases, which hold that the POGG encompasses "the power to incorporate companies with objects other than provincial", "the power to perform Canadian […] treaties" (although later denied in the *Labour Conventions* case),[9] the power to

[3]Hogg 2014, s. 17.2.

[4]Hogg 2014, s. 17.2, 17.3(d). But see Brouillet 2011, at 619, who finds support in the case of *Crown Zellerbach* for the conclusion that newness also plays a role.

[5]See Hogg 2014, s. 17.1.

[6]Perhaps Canada is, after all, more an autonomy arrangement than a federal arrangement. The fact that the Senate does not seem to perform any useful federal function in the Canadian setting would seem to support such a conclusion from an institutional perspective. See also Smith 2010, pp. 74–84, and Inwood 2013, p. 263 f.

[7]Hogg 2014, s. 17.1.

[8]Hogg 2014, s. 17.2.

[9]As explained in Hogg 2014, s. 17.2, the framers of the Constitution Act, 1867 withheld treaty-making powers to the British Empire and did not contemplate the possibility that Canada would, at some future point, "eventually acquire the power to enter into treaties on its own behalf". The so-called *Labour Conventions* case, *A.-G. Can. v. A.-G. Ont.*, [1937] A.C. 326 (in Olmsted 1954, pp. 180–206), however, holds that the federation cannot incorporate in national law by means of federal legislation international treaties that it has concluded without considering the distribution of legislative powers in Sections 91 and 92. Because the federal law that had been enacted for the purpose of incorporating the treaty obligations within the area of labour law intruded into those legislative powers established for provinces in Section 92(13) (property and civil rights in the province), the federal law was unconstitutional for reasons of being *ultra vires*

enact a federal Official Language Act applicable only to federal institutions and agencies,[10] and the power to regulate offshore mineral resources outside the boundaries of each province.[11] "In these cases, the Constitution recognizes certain topics as being classes of subjects for distribution-of-powers purposes, but fails to deal completely with each topic. The p.o.g.g. language completes the incomplete assignment of power. The gap branch of p.o.g.g. covers these limited and unusual cases, where the application of the p.o.g.g. power is almost logically required."[12]

The 'national concern' branch of the POGG power can be defined as "a need for one national law which cannot realistically be satisfied by cooperative provincial action because the failure of one province to cooperate would carry with it adverse consequences for the residents of other provinces".[13] Arguably, this has been the case in some specific situations, such as the regulation of aeronautics,[14] the

the federal legislative powers. Therefore, the federation can use federal law to incorporate treaties within the federal legislative powers of Section 91, but would need the consent of all provinces prior to concluding the treaty for matters that fall within Section 92 or would have file a declaration that limits the treaty to the ambit of Section 92. As explained in Hogg 2014, s. 11.5(c), "[p] rovincial autonomy would be seriously threatened if a treaty made by the federal government could lead to an automatic increase in the legislative authority of the federal Parliament". This case also makes reference to the doctrine of "watertight compartments" between the federal and the provincial legislative powers (see Olmsted 1954, p. 206). The situation would thus be the same as in relation to the Åland Islands between 1920 and 1951 (interestingly coinciding timewise with the *Labour Conventions* case indicating an increasing understanding of the importance of international treaties), when the exercise of treaty powers of Finland systematically resulted in placing legislative competence with the Parliament of Finland. As a consequence of provincial legislative powers in areas also covered by international treaties, it has become necessary to conclude inter-governmental agreements on the observance at the provincial level of the treaties concluded by the federation. See, e.g., Canadian Intergovernmental Agreement Regarding the Implementation of International Labour Cooperation Agreements, at http://www.labour.gc.ca/eng/relations/prov_terr/lca.shtml (accessed on 9 November 2015) and North American Agreement on Labour Cooperation–Canadian Intergovernmental Agreement, at http://www.labour.gc.ca/eng/relations/prov_terr/naalc.shtml (accessed on 9 November 2015). As concerns treaty-making powers of the provinces with third States or other subjects of international law, such an argument can be made, but has never been accepted by the federal government. See Hogg 2014, s. 11.5(c), 11.6, 15.9(f).

[10]As explained in Hogg 2014, s. 17.2, because such entities "are 'clearly beyond provincial reach', they must be within federal reach under the opening p.o.g.g. words of s. 91, 'on the basis of the purely residuary character of the legislative power thereby conferred'".

[11]As explained in Hogg 2014, s. 17.2, offshore minerals were outside each province's legislative jurisdiction and they "therefore had to come within the federal Parliament's p.o.g.g. power 'in its residual capacity'".

[12]Hogg 2014, s. 17.2.

[13]Hogg 2014, s. 17.3(b).

[14]*Johannesson v. Municipality of West St. Paul*, [1952] 1 SCR 292, 1951 CanLII 55 (SCC), p. 328 f.: "[T]he whole subject of aeronautics lies within the field assigned to Parliament as a matter affecting the peace, order and good government of Canada; S. 921 of The Municipal Act (R.S.M. 1940 c. 141) clearly trespasses upon that field and must be declared *ultra vires* the province."

development of the national capital region of Ottawa,[15] the regulation of marine pollution,[16] and the adoption of regulatory measures concerning nuclear power.[17] Very often, situations of this kind flow from the fact that the "failure of one province to act would injure the residents of the other (cooperating) provinces".[18] There is also the requirement of distinctness for the exercise of POGG powers for reasons of national concern, fulfilled in the above-mentioned situations, but not for the attempt to pass federal legislation to regulate consequences of inflation, such as wage and price control, because "inflation was too broad and diffuse a topic to qualify as a 'matter' coming within the national concern branch".[19] Finally, the 'emergency' branch of the POGG powers is mainly geared towards accepting temporally limited federal laws during national exigencies that under normal circumstances would fall under provincial legislative authority.[20] This part of the POGG power was used to justify anti-inflation measures that could not be validated under the national concern branch of POGG,[21] but also for bringing into force the War Measures Act because of perceived insurrection in Quebec in 1970,[22] bringing

[15]*Munro v. National Capital Commission*, [1966] SCR 663, 1966 CanLII 74 (SCC): "That subject matter [development of the national capital region—MS] is not referred to in either s. 91 or s. 92 of the British North America Act. Consequently, the sole power rests with Parliament under the preliminary words of s. 91, relative to 'laws for the peace, order and good government of Canada'. It was therefore within the powers of Parliament to authorize the Commission, for the attainment of its objects and purposes as defined in the Act, to make the expropriation of the lands of the appellant."

[16]*R. v. Crown Zellerbach Canada Ltd.*, [1988] 1 SCR 401, 1988 CanLII 63 (SCC): "A basis for federal legislative jurisdiction to control marine pollution generally in provincial waters cannot be found in any of the specified heads of federal jurisdiction in s. 91 of the Constitution Act, 1867, whether taken individually or collectively." Dumping wastewater in a river that flowed to the Pacific constituted marine pollution, and "because of its predominantly extra provincial as well as international character and implications, is clearly a matter of concern to Canada as a whole". Therefore, the requirement of a dumping licence under the federal Ocean Dumping Control Act "meets the consideration, emphasized by a majority of this Court in the Anti Inflation Act reference, 1976 CanLII 16 (SCC), [1976] 2 S.C.R. 373, that in order for a matter to qualify as one of national concern falling within the federal peace, order and good government power it must have ascertainable and reasonable limits, in so far as its impact on provincial jurisdiction is concerned".

[17]*Ontario Hydro v. Ontario (Labour Relations Board)*, [1993] 3 SCR 327, 1993 CanLII 72 (SCC): "Parliament's exclusive jurisdiction over nuclear electrical generating stations is also founded on its power to legislate over matters of national concern under the peace, order and good government clause in s. 91 of the Constitution Act, 1867. There is no doubt that the production, use and application of atomic energy constitute a matter of national concern, which is predominantly extra-provincial and international in character and implications, and possesses sufficiently distinct and separate characteristics to make it subject to Parliament's residual power."

[18]Hogg 2014, s. 17.3(b).

[19]Hogg 2014, s. 17.3(c). See also Smith 2010, pp. 94–100.

[20]Hogg 2014, s. 17.4(e), 17.5. See also *Re: Anti-Inflation Act*, [1976] 2 SCR 373, 1976 CanLII 16 (SCC).

[21]*Re: Anti-Inflation Act*, [1976] 2 SCR 373, 1976 CanLII 16 (SCC).

[22]As pointed out in Hogg 2014, s. 17.4(c), the constitutionality of the invocation of the War Measures Act was never reviewed by the courts.

into force the War Measures Act in the aftermath of the first world war for reasons of price control,[23] rent control during and after the second world war,[24] and deportation of Japanese Canadians after the second world war.[25] During the evolution of the emergency branch of the POGG power, the federal government has also suffered defeats, such as in attempts to pass legislation to license insurance companies,[26] to regulate hoarding of certain products necessary for life and to price such products,[27] settlement of industrial disputes,[28] and federal prohibition on the manufacture and sale of margarine.[29] However, emergency powers are a particular area of legislative powers and thus not in the main focus in this context.

As concerns the legislative powers of the Finnish Parliament and the Legislative Assembly of the Åland Islands, their exclusive nature in relation to each other is upheld more in the manner of water-tight compartments than as competence areas that allow overlapping. A matter belongs either to the legislative competence of the Parliament or of the Legislative Assembly, and even in situations where an area of legislation is divided between the two law-makers, the dividing line is sharp. This is also reflected in the lists of enumerations in Section 27 and Section 18 of the Self-Government Act: both lists of enumerations are relatively long and detailed. However, at the end of each list, there is a similarly worded provision that aims at distributing to either list such legislative matters that the distinct points in the two enumerations do not cover. In Section 27(42), it is provided that the Parliament of Finland has the legislative powers in "other matters that are deemed to be within the legislative power of the State according to the principles underlying this Act". Conversely, in Section 18(27), it is established that the Legislative Assembly of the Åland Islands shall have legislative powers in respect of "other matters deemed to be within the legislative power of Åland in accordance with the principles underlying this Act". Hence the point of departure is that any matter not mentioned in the listings can, with the help of principles underlying the Self-Government Act, be attributed either to the Parliament or to the Legislative Assembly on the basis of the two "extension clauses" by means of which additional matters can be added to the lists by means of interpretation.

---

[23]See the case of *Fort Frances Pulp and Power Co. v. Man. Free Press Co.* [1923] A.C. 695, as quoted and analyzed in Hogg 2014, s. 17.4(b).

[24]*Reference re Wartime Leasehold Regulations*, [1950] SCR 124, 1950 CanLII 27 (SCC).

[25]See the case of *Co-op. Committee on Japanese Canadians v. A.G. Can.* [1947] A.C. 87, in Olmsted 1954, pp. 458–481, as analyzed in Hogg 2014, s. 17.4(b).

[26]See Hogg 2014, s. 17.4(a).

[27]See the case of *Board of Commerce* [1922] 1 A.C. 191, in Olmsted 1954, pp. 245–254, as quoted and analyzed in Hogg 2014, s. 17.4(a).

[28]See the case of *Toronto Electric Commissioners v. Snider* [1925] A.C. 396, in Olmsted 1954, pp. 394–412, as quoted and analyzed in Hogg 2014, s. 17.4(a). POGG power was unavailable because the object of regulation, relations between employers and employees, "was a matter of civil rights in the province, and therefore within provincial jurisdiction".

[29]See the case of *Can. Federation of Agriculture v. A.G. Que* [1951] A.C. 179, in Olmsted 1954, pp. 665–690, as analyzed in Hogg 2014, s. 17.4(a).

According to the *travaux preparatoires* behind the Self-Government Act,[30] the legislative intention of the relevant paragraphs in Sections 18 and 27 is to establish which matters are part of the competence of the Åland Islands and which matters are part of the competence of mainland Finland. Furthermore, it is stated in the *travaux* that all fields of law have not been mentioned and cannot even be enumerated. The enumerations contain clauses of a general nature, which are to be determinative when legislative competence is delineated, e.g., concerning new fields of law. Ålandic acts are particular acts that have the same effect as acts enacted by the Parliament of Finland. As a consequence, an Ålandic act shall be implemented by courts of law and by other public authorities in the same manner as an act of the Parliament of Finland. The legislative competence of the Åland Islands is exclusive within the fields mentioned in Section 18. As a consequence, acts that have been enacted by the Parliament within these fields are not in effect in the Åland Islands. Moreover, legislative competence of the Åland Islands means that the Legislative Assembly can refrain from regulating fields that are mentioned in the listing of Section 18. Conversely, enactments by the Parliament of Finland within Section 27, as well as decrees issued on the basis of them within the competence of the Parliament, shall also be effective within the Åland Islands.

With a view to the fact that the Legislative Assembly of the Åland Islands is competent to enact legislation mainly within the field of public law, it seems that the principles underlying the Self-Government Act drive the application of Section 18(27) in the direction of public law matters. Because private law matters come under Ålandic competence only to a very limited extent, it can be presumed that a need and opportunity to apply this extension in the sphere of private law will present itself only rarely. For the Parliament of Finland, again, the application of the extension clause in Section 27(42) may be possible in the sphere of public law, save for the fact that the most important areas of public law are allocated to the Åland Islands in Section 18, but in particular in the sphere of private law, which almost in its entirety is within the competence of the Parliament. This distribution of legislative competence on the basis of the extension clauses may appear imbalanced, but it is also possible to argue that there is balance: within the core areas of public law, the extension clause of Section 18(27) operates in favour of the Åland Islands, while in the sphere of private law, the extension clause of Section 27(42) operates in favour of the Parliament.

The two enumerations in the 1991 Self-Government Act, enacted in 1991 and entering into force in 1993, are fresh in comparison with those in the Constitution Act, 1867. Thus the specific heads of power in the 1991 Self-Government Act reflect a relatively modern understanding of issues that could be regulated by law

---

[30]Regeringens proposition RP 73/1990 rd till Riksdagen med förslag till ny självstyrelselag för Åland, pp. 42, 63 f., 73. As pointed out on p. 41, one reason for renewing the distribution of competence in the 1951 Act was the unclear nature of the extent of legislative competence where competence was divided within the same matter, an unclarity that also complicated the application of legislation. The general idea seems to have been to establish a clear distribution of legislative competence in the 1991 Self-Government Act.

(e.g., welfare issues, the environment, etc.), and the passage of time is not yet such that it would have resulted in a need to develop, by means of legal interpretation, a doctrine containing a very varied understanding of different positions. In fact, it may be that a new Self-Government Act will be enacted around 2020–2022. However, the Supreme Court of Finland has had the opportunity in at least four instances to express itself on issues not contemplated by the two enumerations, quite soon after the entering into force of the 1991 Act. At those junctures, the Supreme Court had the opportunity to apply both Section 27(42) and Section 18(27), and thus in practice add new heads of power to either of the lists. In the event, the Supreme Court upheld the rather tight dividing line between the two legislative competences, because the distribution of legislative powers between the Parliament and the Legislative Assembly does not lead to such overlap that either of the two gains a position of supremacy or paramountcy.

While elections are the main mechanism of participation in the governance of the Åland Islands and the direct participation of the population of the Åland Islands by way of referendum is not mentioned in the Self-Government Act, the referendum issue was very much on the agenda when the then pending accession of Finland to the EU in the mid-1990s prompted issues of such magnitude that the need for popular consultation was actualized. With the accession of Finland to the European Union and with the emerging principle of integration by referendum, it was asked whether the Åland Islands should hold an advisory referendum on the EU issue before the Legislative Assembly of the Åland Islands gave its formal consent to the Islands' membership of the EU, which entails special EU status on the basis of a separate protocol on the Åland Islands.[31] The reason for the concerns were that EU law sets aside Ålandic norms and interferes with the jurisdiction of Åland especially within the areas of trade, agriculture and fisheries, and therefore, it could be argued that EU membership would have the effect of diminishing the autonomy of the Åland Islands. Lacking specific referendum provisions, one issue that arose on the basis of the Self-Government Act in this respect was whether the Åland Islands were permitted to organize popular votes of any kind. The Government of the Åland Islands submitted a legislative proposal containing a draft for an act of Åland on an advisory referendum about the EU accession, and the Legislative Assembly passed it. However, during the competence control, doubts were expressed about the power of the Legislative Assembly to enact such a piece of law.

In an Opinion to the President of the Republic, the Supreme Court of Finland emphasized the fact that the referendum would only be advisory, and that it did not constitute any infringement of the decision-making procedures established in the Self-Government Act. Therefore, the advisory referendum did not deprive the Legislative Assembly of its right to represent the Åland Islands. On that basis, the Court found that regulations concerning an advisory referendum did not violate the Self-Government Act. The Court concluded that provisions concerning advisory

[31]The Act concerning the Conditions of Accession and the Adjustments to the Treaties on which the Union is Founded, Protocol No 2 on the Åland Islands, OJ 94/C 241/08.

referendums are not of a constitutional character in the sense that they would, under Section 27(1), deviate from the competence of the Parliament to enact laws at the constitutional level. On the contrary, the Supreme Court ruled that in this case, Ålandic legislation concerning an advisory referendum could be enacted under Section 18(27), because the matter fell under the competence of the Åland Islands.[32] By way of this reference to the "imp lied powers" of the Legislative Assembly to enact an act of Åland which is within the legislative profile of the Åland Islands although not materially enumerated amongst the legislative powers, the advisory referendum was found to be within its competence. As a consequence, the President of Finland did not veto the Act of Åland on the advisory EU referendum and therefore,[33] the referendum could be held.[34]

In the 1990s the Legislative Assembly also proposed to adopt legislation concerning sports activities, which envisaged the delegation of public tasks of an administrative nature to a private entity outside the regular public administration. The Self-Government Act does not contain any explicit provisions about transfer of decision-making powers in administrative matters to organizations that are outside the regular administration of the Åland Islands. The Supreme Court was of the opinion that the general government and administration of the Åland Islands is, on the basis of Section 3(2), the responsibility of the Government of the Åland Islands and those public authorities that are subordinated to the Government. However, the Court concluded that it does not follow from this provision that it is not possible to

[32]Opinion of the Supreme Court, 9 September 1994, Nr 3169 (Dnr OH 94/104).

[33]A decisive referendum would clearly require an amendment of the Self-Government Act. However, the Opinion of the Supreme Court can be criticized for placing too much emphasis on the title of the Act of Åland on the Advisory Referendum concerning the Accession to the European Union, because the question formulated in the Act that would be submitted to the people indicated that the Legislative Assembly would have to vote according to the opinion of the people. Hence the question in the referendum, as established in the Act, gave the impression that the result is binding on the Legislative Assembly, and as a consequence, it could be argued, the law-making powers of the Legislative Assembly would be disturbed in a manner which would require a formal amendment to the Self-Government Act permitting referendums. In the same vein, but in another situation, if the Åland Islanders would like to carry out a referendum on the independence of the Åland Islands by means of a referendum created under an act of Åland, the result would be similar: an act of Åland with norms about an independence referendum would clearly be contrary to section 27, para. 1, of the Self-Government Act and therefore, such a law would be reviewed negatively by the Supreme Court and, as a consequence, be vetoed by the President under section 19(2) of the Self-Government Act on that ground and also because the said act would deal with the external or internal security of the state.

[34]The Ålandic advisory referendum on membership of the EU was organized on 20 November 1994. Only those with the right of domicile had the right to vote in this regional referendum. The EU referendum, the first referendum ever on the Åland Islands and the only one so far, produced a low turnout of only 49.1%. Of those voting, 73.6% voted for the EU, while 26.4% opposed joining the Union together with Finland. The Legislative Assembly of the Åland Islands accordingly made its final decision on 2 December 1994, applying the required two-thirds qualified majority, because Finland's accession to the European Union was made according to the procedure of limited constitutional exceptions, requiring the same qualified majority in the Parliament of Finland for the final decision.

transfer public functions to an organization outside of the regular public administration, quite the contrary: there exist plenty of examples of so-called indirect public administration, including some in the Åland Islands created under Ålandic law. The Supreme Court concluded that because the Åland Islands have, on the basis of Section 18(1), legislative competence concerning the Government of the Åland Islands and the officials and services subordinate to it, the legislative competence should, on the basis of application of Section 18(27), be deemed to belong to the Åland Islands.[35] It is therefore possible to say that indirect public administration through private organizations can be used for the implementation of Ålandic legislation; the competence is not explicit, but is based on an interpretation of Section 18(27), read in conjunction with Section 18(1).

In an Opinion concerning accounting procedures relating to the administration of the Åland Islands,[36] the Supreme Court scrutinized the creation of an entirely new and independent public authority, the Åland Islands Accounting Office, organizationally subordinated to the Legislative Assembly of the Åland Islands. The Court referred to Section 18(1) of the Self-Government Act and made the point that the Åland Islands has legislative competence concerning the organization of the Legislative Assembly and of the Government of the Åland Islands, including officials and services subordinate to the Government. The wording of the provision does not seem to give the Åland Islands any competence to create free-standing and independent authorities or authorities which are subordinated to the Legislative Assembly. In spite of this it may be presumed that the legislative competence of Åland must cover a measure of the kind at hand, where tasks which until this point have been attributed to the Government of the Åland Islands and which only deal with the internal control and supervision of the administration and economy of the Åland Islands, are transferred to a public authority which organizationally is under the Legislative Assembly. Although doubts may arise concerning whether the creation of an independent public authority under the Legislative Assembly can be interpreted as falling under Section 18(1) of the Self-Government Act, the Supreme Court concluded that in this case, the Åland Islands have legislative competence according to Section 18(27) of the Self-Government Act as the circumstances fell within the category of other matters that according to the principles of the Self-Government Act shall be referred to the legislative competence of the Åland Islands. The Court was thus of the opinion that the legislation was within the legislative competence of the Åland Islands.

As concerns incursion into the legislative competence of the Parliament of Finland, the Supreme Court of Finland expressed itself on the Ålandic Act on Application within the Åland Islands of the Parliament's enactments on Gene

[35] Opinion of the Supreme Court Opinion of 19 December 1996. Since the 2000 Constitution of Finland, Section 124 of the Constitution sets out conditions for the transfer of public tasks and public powers to entities that are not identified as public authorities in the Constitution. This provision would also apply to the Legislative Assembly of the Åland Islands in situations where it contemplates the use of so-called indirect public administration for the purposes of implementation of Ålandic legislation.

[36] Opinion of the Supreme Court of 15 February 2013 (Dnr OH2013/18).

Technology and Genetically Modified Organisms.[37] The Court held in its Opinion that legislation on gene technology is not mentioned in the enumerations of Åland's and the Parliament's legislative areas in Sections 18, 27 and 29 of the Self-Government Act. The legislation also cannot be directly attributed to any of the areas mentioned in the enumerations. Therefore, the Court needed to resort to Sections 18(27) and 27(42) to decide the matter on the basis of the underlying principles of the Self-Government Act. According to the Court, gene technology can have an impact on several of the areas within the competence of the Åland Islands, such as the protection of nature and the environment, agriculture and forestry, health care, and animal protection and veterinary functions, which are areas that on the basis of Section 18(10, 12, 15, 17) of the Self-Government Act belong, with some exceptions, to the legislative competence of the Åland Islands. After a review of a great number of legislative competences of the Parliament in Section 27, the Supreme Court held that the Parliament has been reserved legislative competence concerning circumstances that require particular scientific expertise with the relevant public authorities or that can have an impact on the environment and health to a great and unforeseeable extent both in the Åland Islands and outside of the jurisdiction. The Court held that gene technology constitutes a deep incursion in natural evolution. Although gene technology to some extent touches upon areas that belong to the competence of the Åland Islands, the Court held that legislation on gene technology should belong to the competence of the Parliament on the basis of Section 27(42). Therefore, the Court recommended to the President that the legislative decision be vetoed.

It might be expected that for the Faroe Islands, management of issues not mentioned in the enumerations is almost a moot question. Some matters identified in the 2005 Takeover Act require negotiations,[38] while other matters do not, and the enumeration of the legislative powers of the Parliament of Denmark is so short and clear that competence conflicts appear unlikely. It should also be safe to assume in this context that matters not mentioned in any enumeration would more or less automatically be regarded as falling within the legislative competence of the Faroe Islands. This argument is indirectly supported by the fact that the adjudication committee that could be created under Section 6(2) of the 1948 Home Rule Act has never been called together, which as a consequence suggests that no such "hard issues" have emerged that did not find a natural harbour, presumably amongst the legislative competence of the Faroe Islands. Also, the fact that the few court cases which have arisen on the basis of practical application do not contain materials of this nature support the contention that new matter or legislative matter not pinpointed by the enumerations belong to the Faroe Islands.[39]

[37]Opinion of the Supreme Court of 21 March 1996.

[38]See also a comment in Hogg 2014, s. 5.5(c) concerning inter-governmental negotiations as an alternative to judicial review.

[39]For an analysis of five cases (of which only one case on labour law is more clearly relevant for distribution of competence), see á Rógvi 2013, pp. 273–277.

In reality, several competence issues processed by Faroese and Danish authorities have dealt with matters or areas of law not mentioned in the enumerations of List A or List B of the Home Rule Act, which was a relevant consideration prior to the 2005 Takeover Act. As early as 1950, the Legislative Assembly enacted a law on mortgaging of cargo of fishing vessels without an actual basis in the fisheries provisions in List A. However, after later amendments to Danish law where the mortgage rules were moved from one piece of law to another, the issue seems to have landed in Danish legislation of a kind that could be viewed as being within Faroese competence. Here, changes in the overall legislative environment in Denmark seem to have facilitated Faroese competence, but it is interesting that the Legislative Assembly of the Faroe Islands has itself been willing to doubt its own competence in a manner that results in internal competence control of some sort. In 1981, the Faroese government submitted a proposal to the Legislative Assembly concerning registers of public authorities, which would apply also to Danish authorities in the Faroe Islands, but after the Danish representative to the Faroe Islands pointed out the inconsistency, the applicability on Danish authorities was removed from the proposal while it was dealt with in the Legislative Assembly. In 1970, after a decade of preparations, a proposal was submitted to the Legislative Assembly on law on the names of persons, but the legislative committee of the Assembly came to the conclusion that legislation on names was not mentioned on List A or List B of the Home Rule Act, and therefore, the matter could not be transferred to the Faroe Islands, which meant that the proposal was not carried in the Legislative Assembly. In 1990, however, the Ministry of Justice of Denmark interpreted the Home Rule Act so that it permitted the transfer of competence in the area of names to the Faroe Islands, which may be regarded an extensive interpretation. This area was finally transferred in 1992.[40]

In addition, safety at sea, an area heavily influenced by international agreements, is not mentioned in either in List A or List B, although some adjacent areas exist in them, such as working conditions, harbours, protection of coasts and registration of ships. Proposals in 1949, 1958, 1973, and 1982 to establish Faroese control of ships within Faroese legislative competence were turned down by the Legislative Assembly, at least once on the basis of discussions with Danish authorities. However, in 1998, an agreement was reached between Danish and Faroese authorities that control of ships would be taken over by the Faroe Islands after further negotiations between the Danish and Faroese governments, which took place in 2001. As with the legislation on names, legislative competence over the control of ships was transferred without explicit basis in the two lists of the Home Rule Act, but on the basis of an agreement between the two governments.[41] With the 2005 Takeover Act, the Danish system has become even less bound to the formal enumerations in the Home Rule Act in a manner that would seem to lead to an assumption of competence on the Faroese side, provided that the Legislative

[40]Rasmussen 2002, pp. 377–379.

[41]Rasmussen 2002, pp. 379–380.

Assembly makes a decision to that effect either with or without negotiations. It should therefore be relatively easy for the law-maker of the Faroe Islands to pick up new legislative matters, as long as there is no transgression into the enumeration of the Danish Parliament.

However, the matter is perhaps not quite this straight forward. The *travaux preparatoires* to the 2005 Takeover Act consider it possible that general social and technological development could result in the emergence of new fields of law where no legal rules currently exist. Therefore, if such a new field of law can be understood as a natural part of a field of law that has already been taken over on the basis of Section 2(1) of the Takeover Act, then the interpretation should be that also the new field of law is overtaken by the Faroese authorities. The same mechanism should exist in relation to fields of law taken over on the basis of Section 2(2).[42] By implication, this would seem to mean that if no natural connection to an existing Faroese field of law can be identified, the new field of law would fall within the competence of the Parliament of Denmark, at least if there is a natural connection to a field of law still within the competence of the Parliament of Denmark. Of course, the Faroe Islands could, in such a situation, decide to transfer the old matter from the Parliament of Denmark to the Legislative Assembly solely in order to claim the new matter.

As explained above, in some instances the existing material enumerations of competences are not able to provide all the answers, and for such instances, the Constitution of Canada contains the possibility for the federation to legislate for peace, order and good government, while for the Åland Islands, the two orders of governments can rely on their respective extension clauses implementing underlying principles of legislative competence in the Self-Government Act. For the Faroe Islands, the easy assumption of competence by the Legislative Assembly can in such situations probably be viewed as a presumption of competence of the Faroe Islands, provided that a natural relationship to an existing field of competence can be established.

References

á Rógvi K (2013) West-nordic constitutional judicial review. Djøf Publishing, Copenhagen

Brouillet E (2011) Canadian Federalism and the principle of subsidiarity: should we open the pandora's box. Supreme Court Law Rev 54 (2):601

Hogg PW (2014) Constitutional law of Canada, 5th edn supplemented, vols 1 and 2. Thomson & Carswell, Toronto [NB! References to Hogg 2014 are to sections in the supplemented loose-leaf volume, not to pages.]

Inwood GJ (2013) Understanding Canadian Federalism—an introduction to theory and practice. Pearson, Toronto

[42]Forslag til Lov om de færøske myndigheders overtagelse af sager og sagsområder, fremsat den 11. maj 2005 af statsministeren (Anders Fogh Rasmussen), section 3.2.1.

Olmsted RA (ed) (1954) Decisions of the judicial committee of the privy council, vol III. Department of Justice, Ottawa
Rasmussen S (2002) Til hjemmestyreloven os skiller. Ugeskrift for Retsvæsen, nr. 43, 26. oktober 2002, pp 377–383
Regeringens Proposition RP 73/1990 rd till Riksdagen med förslag till ny självstyrelselag för Åland
Smith DE (2010) Federalism and the constitution of Canada. University of Toronto Press, Toronto

Chapter 6
Excursus: The European Union

From its early days, the European Union or, as it first was called, the European Economic Community and the European Community, has tried to come to terms with its relationship with the Member States by establishing a federal-like distribution of legislative competences and by defining itself as an independent legal order based on the notion of primacy of Community law.[1] With successive amendments to the constitutive treaties, an understanding evolved that a competence creep from the Community in the direction of the Member States was taking place: the Community was increasingly legislating in areas that had traditionally been understood as the remit of the Member States. By the turn of the millennium, the structure of the European Union became the target of political discussions with a view to reforming the EU.

In the European Commission, the restructuring of the EU was prepared on the basis of a White Paper, in which the Commission stated, *inter alia*, the following:[2] "The Union needs clear principles identifying how competence is shared between the Union and its Member States. In the first place this is to respond to the public's frequent question 'who does what in Europe?' A common vision is needed to

[1]See *Costa v. Enel*, 15 July 1964, Case 6/641 [1], mentioned in the particular declaration attached by the inter-governmental conference to the TEU and the TFEU (17. Declaration concerning primacy): "The Conference recalls that, in accordance with well settled case law of the Court of Justice of the European Union, the Treaties and the law adopted by the Union on the basis of the Treaties have primacy over the law of Member States, under the conditions laid down by the said case law. The Conference has also decided to attach as an Annex to this Final Act the Opinion of the Council Legal Service on the primacy of EC law as set out in 11197/07 (JUR 260): 'Opinion of the Council Legal Service of 22 June 2007—It results from the case-law of the Court of Justice that primacy of EC law is a cornerstone principle of Community law. According to the Court, this principle is inherent to the specific nature of the European Community. At the time of the first judgment of this established case law (Costa/ENEL, 15 July 1964, Case 6/641 [1]) there was no mention of primacy in the treaty. It is still the case today. The fact that the principle of primacy will not be included in the future treaty shall not in any way change the existence of the principle and the existing case-law of the Court of Justice.'"

[2]*European Governance—a White Paper*. Brussels, 25.7.2001, COM(2001) 428 final, p. 34 f.

M. Suksi, *Double Enumeration of Legislative Powers in a Sub-State Context*, SpringerBriefs in Law, https://doi.org/10.1007/978-3-319-90921-9_6

answer this question. The White Paper has highlighted a tangible Europe that is in full development; a Union based on multi-level governance in which each actor contributes in line with his or her capabilities or knowledge to the success of the overall exercise. In a multi-level system the real challenge is establishing clear rules for how competence is shared—not separated; only that non-exclusive vision can secure the best interests of all the Member States and all the Union's citizens." The clarification of the legislative roles of the EU and the Member States thus did not entail a separation of legislative competences that would have been based on two lists of exclusive competences. Here, the Commission makes clear that the intention is not to separate the legislative competences of the EU and the Member State, but rather to find new ways to share them.

In the so-called Laeken Declaration on the Future of the European Union,[3] which the White Paper of the Commission preceded and prepared, the importance of clarifying, simplifying and adjusting the division of competences between the Union and the Member States in the light of the new challenges facing the Union was underlined. The Laeken Declaration, which can be understood as a starting point for the major constitutional overhaul of EU structures, both institutional and material, during the first decade of the 21st century, made the point that the reform could "lead both to restoring tasks to the Member States and to assigning new missions to the Union, or to the extension of existing powers, while constantly bearing in mind the equality of the Member States and their mutual solidarity". A clearer distinction between three types of competence was looked for: "the exclusive competence of the Union, the competence of the Member States and the shared competence of the Union and the Member States." The aim was to find out at which one of the two levels of governance, the EU or the Member State, competence is exercised in the most efficient way and how the principle of subsidiarity influences the distribution of powers. Most importantly, the following questions were posed: "And should we not make it clear that any powers not assigned by the Treaties to the Union fall within the exclusive sphere of competence of the Member States? And what would be the consequences of this?"

As a result of the above preparatory work, reorganisation of the competences was on the table at the Convention assembled in 2002–2003 to review the constitutional structure of the EU, to the extent that there were queries as to whether or not the Member States should be provided with guarantees that their spheres of competence would not be affected. Further, it was questioned "how to ensure that a redefined division of competence does not lead to a creeping expansion of the competence of the Union" or to "encroachment upon the exclusive areas of competence of the Member States and, where there is provision for this, regions".[4] However, in spite of reference to the exclusive areas of competence of Member

---

[3]European Union document SN 273/01 of 15 December 2001.

[4]Laeken Declaration on the Future of the European Union (15 December 2001), at https://www.cvce.eu/en/obj/laeken_declaration_on_the_future_of_the_european_union_15_december_2001-en-a76801d5-4bf0-4483-9000-e6df94b07a55.html (accessed on 31 January 2018).

States, it is likely that no system of double enumeration, one for the EU and another for the Member States, was seriously discussed in the Convention of 2002–2003. This method of distribution of competence was therefore probably not on the table, either, in the ensuing 2003–2004 inter-governmental conference that finalised the abortive constitutional treaty, nor dealt with in the 2007 inter-governmental conference that resulted in the so-called Lisbon Treaty of the EU in 2009, the provisions of which make up the Treaty on European Union (TEU) and the Treaty on the Functioning of the European Union (TFEU). What was debated was how the competences of the EU, not of the Member States, should be fashioned: "In the Convention, the idea of establishing a precise and rigid catalogue of competences was discussed but quickly abandoned: it was found to be too difficult to establish and, in any case, inappropriate, given the characteristics of the EU."[5]

As a consequence, Article 4(1) TEU states that "[i]n accordance with Article 5, competences not conferred upon the Union in the Treaties remain with the Member States", indicating a residual competence for the Member States. This is confirmed in Article 5(2) of the TEU, according to which "the Union shall act only within the limits of the competences conferred upon it by the Member States in the Treaties to attain the objectives set out therein. Competences not conferred upon the Union in the Treaties remain with the Member States." In addition, Articles 2 through 6 of the TFEU specify the range of action of the EU, from exclusive competences[6] via shared competences[7] to supporting competences,[8] including an area of parallel competences of the EU and Member States where no preemption of national competences by EU law applies,[9] defined in greater detail in the material provisions of Articles 26 through 197 of the TFEU. However, no listing of exclusive competences of the Member States is indicated in the two treaties. The method of distribution of legislative competence in the EU is therefore essentially of a federal

---

[5]Piris 2010, p. 76.

[6]According to Article 3(1), the Union shall have exclusive competence in the following areas: customs union; the establishing of the competition rules necessary for the functioning of the internal market; monetary policy for the Member States whose currency is the euro; the conservation of marine biological resources under the common fisheries policy; and common commercial policy. In addition, according to Article 3(2), the EU has treaty-making powers in these areas.

[7]According to Article 4(2), shared competence between the EU and the Member States applies in the following principal areas: internal market; social policy, for the aspects defined in this Treaty; economic, social and territorial cohesion; agriculture and fisheries, excluding the conservation of marine biological resources; environment; consumer protection; transport; trans-European networks; energy; area of freedom, security and justice; and common safety concerns in public health matters, for the aspects defined in the TFEU.

[8]According to Article 6, these competences are the following: protection and improvement of human health; industry; culture; tourism; education, vocational training, youth and sport; civil protection; and administrative cooperation. See Piris 2010, p. 74 f.

[9]The parallel competences mentioned in Article 4(3) and 4(4) are the following: research; technological development; space; development cooperation; and humanitarian aid. See Rosas and Armati 2012, p. 24: "In these areas, the Union has competence to carry out activities but the exercise of that competence shall not result in Member States being prevented from exercising theirs."

nature, with enumerated powers held by the EU and residual powers held by the Member States.[10] However, a hint as to some of the competences of the Member States is provided for in Article 6 of the TFEU, according to which the Union shall have competence to carry out actions to support, coordinate or supplement the actions of the Member States in certain areas, namely, protection and improvement of human health; industry; culture; tourism; education, vocational training, youth and sport; civil protection; and administrative cooperation.

Of these particularly culture, tourism, education, and youth, but potentially also vocational training and sport,[11] stand out as competence areas not mentioned amongst the material competences of the EU as according strong legislative powers to the EU, as the possibility of harmonisation of the laws and regulations of the Member States in these areas is excluded. In Article 165(1) TFEU on education, vocational training, youth and sport there is a further caveat that "while fully respecting the responsibility of the Member States for the content of teaching and the organisation of education systems and their cultural and linguistic diversity", the EU shall contribute to the development of quality education by encouraging cooperation between Member States and, if necessary, supporting and supplementing the action of Member States. Although some of these powers are not actually conferred on the EU as legislative competences, it would be bold to suggest that these areas constitute a positive listing of competences of the Member State that the EU cannot legislate within.

Furthermore, the material provisions of the TFEU contain specific language that confers law-making competence on the Union concerning human health and industry. Given the structure of the legal order of the EU and the primacy accorded to it along the principles established in the case of *Costa v. Enel*,[12] it therefore seems that even the areas of culture, tourism, education and youth cannot be presented as exclusive competences of the Member States where the Union would never legislate. The primacy of EU law constitutes a permanent supremacy principle for EU law in relation to the law of the Member States in a manner that can materialize in almost any area of law within the residual competence of the Member State, provided that the law-maker of the EU is able to establish a legal basis in the treaties for its legislative action.

At the same time, it is clear that the TEU and the TFEU do not confer all possible types of legislative competence on the EU (not even under conditions where the so-called implied powers can be applied on the basis of Article 352 TFEU). Therefore, legislative areas that do not belong to the policy areas conferred to the EU, for example typical sovereignty-related issues such as elections to the national parliament, should remain outside the remit of the EU legislator. The point here is simply that it is not possible to know exactly what these areas are, and it

---

[10]Probably partly for this reason, it is possible for Piris 2010, p. 331, to state the following: "The Lisbon Treaty did not change the nature of the Union, which remains a partially federal entity."

[11]Sport can be both an employment and business, which are EU competences.

[12]*Costa v E.N.E.L.* (Case 6/64) [1964] ECR 1203.

would probably have been next to impossible for the Member States to agree on an enumeration of exclusive legislative competences of the Member States during the various inter-governmental conferences leading up to the current distribution of legislative powers in the EU. The focus being less on the exclusive competences of the EU (which are relatively clear), the shared competences of the EU is the problematic field: the "battle" about who occupies the shared competence, the EU or the Member States, will continue, and it will "be difficult in many areas for the Member States to exercise their powers in a manner compatible with the plethora of existing EU rules".[13] The question—and at this point of the evolution of the EU perhaps a merely rhetorical one—that can be asked from the point of view of double enumeration is whether an additional definition of exclusive competences of the Member States would have solidified the position of the Member States and stemmed the competence creep?[14]

Against the background of the Canadian model of federalism, it should be possible to give a positive answer to that question, at least from a formal legal point of view, but there may still have been extra-legal ways to persuade Member States to carry out various tasks, namely by using the financial leverage, also present in the Canadian context, that the EU has. However, if it was to be present, such a formulation of a double enumeration for the EU should probably have been achieved at the very beginning of European integration in the 1950s; it was probably too late to introduce an enumeration for the Member States in the first decade of the 2000s.

The move with the 1951 Self-Government Act of Åland from a single enumeration of the Parliament of Finland to a double enumeration of the legislative competences so that also the Legislative Assembly of the Åland Islands was assigned specific legislative competencies does, of course, at least in principle confirm that it is possible to move from a single enumeration to a double

[13]Rosas and Armati 2012, p. 25.

[14]There is a declaration by the inter-governmental conference (18. Declaration in relation to the delimitation of competences) to that effect attached to the TEU and the TFEU: "The Conference underlines that, in accordance with the system of division of competences between the Union and the Member States as provided for in the Treaty on European Union and the Treaty on the Functioning of the European Union, competences not conferred upon the Union in the Treaties remain with the Member States. When the Treaties confer on the Union a competence shared with the Member States in a specific area, the Member States shall exercise their competence to the extent that the Union has not exercised, or has decided to cease exercising, its competence. The latter situation arises when the relevant EU institutions decide to repeal a legislative act, in particular better to ensure constant respect for the principles of subsidiarity and proportionality. The Council may, at the initiative of one or several of its members (representatives of Member States) and in accordance with Article 241 of the Treaty on the Functioning of the European Union, request the Commission to submit proposals for repealing a legislative act. The Conference welcomes the Commission's declaration that it will devote particular attention to these requests. Equally, the representatives of the governments of the Member States, meeting in an Intergovernmental Conference, in accordance with the ordinary revision procedure provided for in Article 48(2) to (5) of the Treaty on European Union, may decide to amend the Treaties upon which the Union is founded, including either to increase or to reduce the competences conferred on the Union in the said Treaties."

enumeration even after the system of distribution of legislative competences has been instituted. In addition, the Faroe Islands arrangement is further proof of the possibility of change concerning the point of departure of enumeration. It should thus not be entirely ruled out that at some point of the evolution of the European Union, political will for such an amendment of the EU treaties might emerge.

It is nonetheless possible to say that there exists an embryonic form of double enumeration in the primary law of the European Union, but of a very diffuse kind: the treaties themselves, as well as the accession treaties, formulate several exceptions to EU law in the area of legislative competence. For instance, as concerns the economic and monetary union, Denmark and the UK have opted out from the general system of joint currency and central bank (see below), established in the Treaty on European Union, while Denmark has certain exemptions regarding purchase by non-nationals of real property for second homes established in Protocol (No 32) on the Acquisition of Property in Denmark. For Finland, Protocol 2 on the Åland Islands, annexed to the accession treaty of Finland, creates a territorial exemption for the Åland Islands in the area of indirect taxes (where the legislative competence is with the Parliament of Finland), regional citizenship in Åland and the right of legal persons to acquire and hold real property on the Åland Islands without permission by the competent authorities of the Åland Islands. In addition, it is possible to maintain restrictions, on a non-discriminatory basis, on the right of establishment and the right to provide services by natural persons who do not enjoy regional citizenship in Åland, or by legal persons without permission of the competent authorities of the Åland Islands. For all these Åland-related matters, legislative competence is reserved to Finland as a Member State, making possible legislation either by the Parliament of Finland or by the Legislative Assembly of the Åland Islands, depending on where the legislative powers are allocated by the 1991 Self-Government Act. Within the former category, examples are the 1975 Act on the Acquisition of Real Property in the Åland Islands[15] and the 1996 Act on Exceptions for the Åland Islands concerning Legislation on Value Added Tax and Excise Duties,[16] both enacted by the Parliament of Finland, while an example within the latter category is the 1996 Ålandic Act on the Right to Carry Out Business.[17]

Accession treaties can also contain exemptions from the application of EU law, as is the case with the Accession treaty of Sweden, which contains a permanent exemption from the prohibition of oral tobacco (snuff) that is in effect elsewhere in the EU on the basis of the tobacco directive of the EU. On the basis of the exemption, the 1993 Tobacco Act of Sweden contains provisions concerning

[15]Jordförvärvslag för Åland (3/1975). On the basis of this Act, the Legislative Assembly of the Åland Islands has enacted legislation that specifies the procedures further. See the Ålandic Act (2003:68) on the Right to Acquire Real Property and on the Permit to Acquire Real Property.

[16]Lag om undantag för landskapet Åland i fråga om mervärdesskatte-och accislagstiftningen (1266/1996).

[17]Landskapslag (1996:47) om rätt att utöva näring.

snuff,[18] which is a legal product within the jurisdiction of Sweden and can be regulated on the basis of the legislative competence of the Parliament of Sweden. There are also other Member States of the EU that have exemptions from EU law at the level of primary law which make possible optouts of various kinds.[19]

An area where "enumeration" of national legislative powers is particularly tangible is monetary policy and central banks. According to Protocol (No 15) on Certain Provisions Relating to the United Kingdom of Great Britain and Northern Ireland, annexed to the TEU and the TFEU, the UK is under no obligation to adopt the euro as currency and shall retain its powers in the field of monetary policy according to national law. Additionally, most of the of the Protocol on the Statute of the European System of Central Banks and of the European Central Bank shall not apply to the United Kingdom. This means, for instance, that the UK Parliament has the enumerated power to enact legislation that institutes the pound sterling as the UK currency as provided for in the UK Currency Act 1982 and maintains the Bank of England as the central bank of the UK as provided for in the UK Bank of England Act 1998.

Somewhat similarly, Protocol (No 16) on Certain Provisions Relating to Denmark makes it possible for Denmark, on the basis of a notice given on 3 November 1993 that Denmark does not intend to participate in the third stage of economic and monetary union, to receive an exemption from all Articles and provisions of the Treaties and the Statute of the ESCB that refer to a derogation.[20] However, Denmark could choose to withdraw its notification and start to participate in the third stage of the monetary union. Until such time, the Parliament of Denmark has its full powers to enact legislation on currency and the Danish Central Bank, currently established in the 1988 Currency Act, where Section 1 establishes that the currency is the crown (*krone*).[21] In addition, the Parliament also has the power to legislate on the Danish Central Bank, which according to Section 1 of the 1936 Act on the Danish National Bank has the task of maintaining a trustworthy currency system and of leading and regulating the circulation of money and granting of credit.[22] In addition, under Section 8(1), the Danish National Bank has the right to issue paper bills.

---

[18]See Tobakslag (1993:581), which applies generally to tobacco products, but contains a specific rule concerning snuff in Section 9a(3), according to which the prohibition in the Act to make reference to taste, smell or additives does not apply to snuff.

[19]It deserves to be mentioned that neither the Faroe Islands nor Greenland are parts of the European Union, although Denmark is a Member State. The Faroe Islands has a fisheries agreement and a free trade agreement with the EU. When Denmark joined the European Economic Community, Greenland became a part of the EEC, but in 1985, a withdrawal of Greenland from the EEC occurred on the basis of negotiations between Denmark and the EEC.

[20]In addition, the Protocol (No 17) on Denmark exempts Denmark from the obligation to subject the Danish Central Bank to the European System of Central Banks according to Article 14 of the Statute of the European Central Bank in relation to those parts of Denmark that are not part of the European Union (which are the Faroe Islands and Greenland).

[21]Lov nr. 817 af 21. december 1988 om Møntlov.

[22]Lov nr 116 af 07/04/1936 om Danmarks Nationalbank.

Hence in spite of the fact that the distribution of legislative powers in the European Union features a federal-like set-up with enumerated powers with the EU and residual powers with the Member States, there exists a patchwork of enumerations of different kinds that allocate legislative powers in some matters to some Member States. This resembles the method of double enumeration, although it is not systematic in relation to all Member States, but instead very unsystematic and mainly in relation to each Member State individually. The reasons for the creation of the scattered national enumerations are tied to the success of prospective Member State during accession negotiations in securing national arrangements that deviate from the general rules of the European Union. The emergence of a patchwork of enumeration for Member States is thus a consequence of political decisions made during the negotiations between the applicant State and the EU about the conditions of accession and reflect the importance of the matter for the individual Member State. Whether all Member States could agree on a joint list of enumerated matters is another matter, as pointed out above. Therefore, it is possible to say that the European Union displays a slight modification of single enumeration towards double enumeration, but clearly without crossing the border from the former to the latter.

References

Piris JC (2010) The Lisbon treaty—a legal and political analysis. Cambridge University Press, Cambridge

Rosas A, Armati L (2012) EU constitutional law—an introduction. Hart Publishing, Oxford and Portland, Oregon

Chapter 7
Concluding Remarks

The duality of legislative competences, fashioned in two enumerations of powers exclusive to each other, reveals through this examination an astounding richness in the ways constitutional law responds to needs of two orders of government. It is, on the basis of this review, possible to construct a category of countries which operate on the basis of dual lists of competences, exclusive in relation to each other, in a manner that distinguishes them from regular federations, on the one hand, and from autonomy arrangements, on the other, where a single list of enumeration is the ordinary point of departure. A double enumeration of legislative competences is clearly a viable option when government is organized, and it appears that this option has, in the three countries studied, not been the initial option, but rather a result of a more or less contentious historical development, in Canada in the decades preceding 1867, in Finland in the time between 1920 and 1951, and in the Faroe Islands in the period from the end of the 1940s until 2005.

Within this group displaying duality of legislative competences significant variations in approach can be detected along a number of dimensions. Canada appears to be a relatively rigid system with few formal changes during the past 150 years, but in reality, constitutional interpretation, in particular the dynamic interpretation of more recent times, has modified the distribution of legislative powers. In Finland, changes have been made according to needs that have arisen, but in principle the system is quite rigid and dependent upon formal amendments to the Self-Government Act for modifications, although a pith and substance thinking is discernible in the Opinions of the Supreme Court. Denmark is the most flexible system in this respect, perhaps at least in part because ordinary law is used as the fundament for the arrangement, which means that it can, in theory, be rolled back by simple majority. It therefore appears that on a dimension of rigidity and flexibility, the Finnish arrangement with respect to the Åland Islands stands out as the most rigid, established in the detailed enumerations of the 1991 Self-Government Act, while the Canadian arrangement seems less rigid due to the dynamism that has emerged through the interpretations of the Supreme Court. The Danish arrangement concerning the Faroe Islands, displays surprising flexibility in the distribution of

M. Suksi, *Double Enumeration of Legislative Powers in a Sub-State Context*, SpringerBriefs in Law, https://doi.org/10.1007/978-3-319-90921-9_7

legislative competences, almost to the point of making it entirely political as to its operation.

This characterisation of the three situations as to their rigidity or flexibility is at least in part explained by the method of distribution of legislative competences, which in the case of Finland and the Åland Islands is based on amendments of the two lists, in the main by use of the method for constitutional amendments, supplemented by the requirement of consent of a qualified majority of two-thirds of the Legislative Assembly of the Åland Islands (but with the exception that according to Section 29 of the Self-Government Act, a few of the competences of the Parliament of Finland, listed in a short enumeration, could be transferred by ordinary legislation of the Parliament). In Canada, some constitutional amendments to the powers of the federation and the provinces have been carried out, but in the main, the two enumerations of powers remain in their original form, while being affected by the interpretations of the Canadian courts, in particular the Supreme Court, as to the material contents of the legislative competences. In addition to the two enumerations of powers, some limited areas of concurrent jurisdiction (not to be confused with concurrent application of law) can be found in the Canadian system, mainly so that priority is, in cases of conflict, given to federal law, but there is also in one instance a reverse concurrency, where the law of a province is given priority over federal law. In Denmark, the distribution of legislative competences between the Parliament and the Faroe Islands is not established in the Constitution, but in ordinary law enacted on the basis of agreements between the two entities, resulting in an arrangement where the Faroe Islands can relatively freely decide to transfer competence by legislative (and thus political) decisions from the Parliament of Denmark to the Faroe Islands. Although this system does not appear to have the same constitutional protection as the other two systems, the agreement between Denmark and the Faroe Islands underlying the arrangement can be viewed as a relatively good assurance of constitutional nature.

As explained above, the purpose of double enumerations is to attribute exclusive legislative competences to two different orders of government. In the three countries reviewed here, this distribution of legislative competences produces three different outcomes. For Finland and the Åland Islands, the outcome can be characterized as a separation of competences, virtually to the degree of creating watertight compartments between the spheres of competence, albeit with certain modifications in the direction of pith and substance thinking. Although the Canadian enumerations are explicitly defined as exclusive in the relevant constitutional provisions, constitutional evolution, in particular the evolution of interpretations by the Supreme Court of Canada, has produced an outcome which can be characterized as cohabitation of competences. In this setting, the two legislative competences are in constant contact with each other and produce, from time to time, overlap that is tolerated. Although exclusivity is the starting point, the fringes of the legislative powers of one order of government can be affected by the powers of the other as long as the core areas of each head of power are preserved. Finally, in Denmark, the outcome of the double enumeration strategy is re-distribution of competences on the basis of political and legislative decisions in the Faroe Islands, possibly in some respects to the point of making the Faroese legislative competences residual.

What is significant in the context of comparison with ordinary federations is that the distribution of legislative competence in the three countries does not operate under any general supremacy clause or preemption doctrine that would, in all situations of normative conflict between national and sub-state legislation, give the upper hand to national law. Exclusivity of the two spheres of power means that generally speaking, one order of government cannot compel the other, which means that the national government in the three countries cannot produce legislation that as a general rule would act to set aside sub-state legislation. The responses in the three countries are different, and the result is a preservation of the legislative sovereignty of each order of government, each within its own competence.

For Finland and the Åland Islands, the outcome is a binary system used to allocate matters once and for all to each order of government, to the extent that if a normative vacuum exists in the legal order of the Åland Islands, it cannot be filled by application of norms in ordinary legislation that the Parliament of Finland has enacted. When issues emerge that do not fall into any of the enumerated heads of power either for the Parliament of Finland or the Åland Islands, the correct legislator is determined on the basis of the two extension clauses at the end of each competence list that distribute competence either to the national Parliament or to the Legislative Assembly of the Åland Islands on the basis of the principles underlying the Self-Government Act. From a practical point of view, the shift in strategy concerning the distribution of legislative powers between Finland and Åland in the transition from the 1920 Self-Government Act to the 1951 Self-Government Act was probably not very dramatic, but from the point of view of principle, the change was of great importance, because a preemption of a kind was built into the 1920 Self-Government Act which was eradicated in the Act of 1951.

Generally speaking, therefore, it is not always beneficial to operate under the assumption that a residual competence for the sub-state entity is a better option, because such a "residual" point of departure may open up the need to recognize or accept a window for national preemption, which in turn can endanger the autonomy of the sub-state entity. In Canada, the response was from the beginning the implementation of exclusive enumerations, making either the federal Parliament or the provincial legislatures competent, but in addition to this, the Canadian Supreme Court has developed a paramountcy option of last resort that may, in some limited situations, give priority to federal law in situations of concurrent application (which should not be confused with concurrent jurisdiction but is a description of what happens when an instance in real life has a so-called double aspect which both orders of legislators try to regulate at the same time). In addition, the opening paragraph of the federal enumeration of legislative competence contains a relatively well-circumscribed entitlement for the federation to legislate for the peace, order and good government of Canada. The Canadian version of the double enumeration strategy thus contains some mitigating factors that soften the edges of the two enumerations, although the enumerations still clearly display exclusivity. The distribution of legislative powers between the Danish Parliament and the Legislative

Assembly of the Faroe Islands is, in this context and in comparison, somewhat confusing, but it seems that the agreement between the two entities underlying the arrangement contains the idea that the Danish Parliament will not legislate for the Faroe Islands within the matters that the Faroese law-maker has received or has decided to take over from the Danish Parliament.

In spite of the creation of two exclusive spheres of legislative competence, or perhaps precisely for that reason, mechanisms of competence control have been put in place to make sure that the law-makers stay within their respective fields of competence. In Canada, competence control is symmetrical in that it covers both the federal and the provincial law-maker: any legislative decision of the two orders of government, federal or provincial, can be challenged before the courts of law as to their compliance with the distribution of legislative power. In Finland, competence control as to legislative action for the territory of the Åland Islands is asymmetrical, because the enactments of the Legislative Assembly of the Åland Islands are controlled as to their conformity with the Ålandic enumeration (and as to their potential transgression into the Parliament's enumeration) by the Åland Delegation and—in some cases—also the Supreme Court, before the President of Finland makes her or his determination on whether the law is within Ålandic competence. At the same time, however, the Constitutional Committee of the Parliament of Finland has not felt itself prevented from considering whether enactments of the Parliament of Finland that have relevance within the territory of the Åland Islands are within the competence of the Parliament. Although this asymmetrical system of competence control has worked surprisingly well, it is in many ways confusing and illogical. The Danish system, which so far has not been used even once since 1948, is unilateral, because only the enactments of the Legislative Assembly of the Faroe Islands can be tried before the adjudication committee as to whether they are within Faroese competence. In addition to the main mechanisms of competence control in Denmark and Finland, application of law in concrete cases before courts could produce choice of law situations, but these are not really instances of competence control proper, established within those systems. In fact, the Danish court system and the few concrete cases that exist signal a wish to avoid consideration of competence issues in the courts.

Competence control can also assume some other characteristics, such as being systematic or unsystematic. As concerns the enactments of the Legislative Assembly of the Åland Islands, competence control can be said to be systematic, because all laws enacted are submitted for such control to the Åland Delegation. However, only a small portion of the laws end up before the Supreme Court of Finland, namely those where the Åland Delegation has found a problem and those which open up a new issue for legislative action. At the same time, it should be pointed out that the conformity of national law with the enumeration of the Finnish Parliament is not systematically controlled by the Constitutional Committee of the Parliament, but only when specific situations arise. For the legislation of the Faroe Islands, the competence control is unsystematic in the sense that not all pieces of law enacted by the Legislative Assembly undergo competence control by the adjudication committee; in fact, no Faroese law has ever been submitted for competence control before the adjudication committee. In addition, no particular system has been created for competence control of national legislation in relation to Faroese law. Instead, competence is from time to time controlled within the framework of political processes, either between the governments of Denmark and the Faroe Islands or within the Legislative Assembly of the Faroe Islands. In Canada, too, the competence control is unsystematic in that each piece of law passed either at the federal or the provincial level does not undergo competence control, only the ones brought to court for, *inter alia*, such control.

However, the characterisation as unsystematic of competence control in at least two of the three countries does not mean that the competence line is not paid attention to; on the contrary, the drafting agencies, which are often departments or ministries of justice or similar entities both within the national government and the sub-state government, keep track of the competence line and draft legislation accordingly. For instance in Canada, the departments of justice either at the federal level or the provincial level assess the competence issue in relation to draft laws. In Denmark, the Parliament regularly inserts a clause amongst the final provisions of an act that the piece of law does not apply to the Faroe Islands, while the Legislative Assembly of the Faroe Islands may refrain from enacting a piece of law for lack of competence. This indicates that an "administrative" competence control takes place prior to the passing of a law, as opposed to the formal control that the Constitutional Committee of the Parliament of Finland performs on the basis of Section 74 of the Constitution of Finland.

Double enumerations of legislative powers introduce an intuitive sense of rigidity even when considering the possibility of opting out from some parts of the arrangement. From the point of view of principle, opting out is probably quite difficult to handle in federal contexts, where the federal arrangement is normally expected to be symmetrical in relation to the constituent states and their powers, but for instance in the European Union, opting out often occurs at the level of primary law, both in the treaties constituting the EU and in the accession treaties of various countries, such as in Protocol 2 on the Åland Islands in the accession treaty of Finland. Such exceptions for Member States concerning the application of EU law may be understood as an embryonic form of double enumeration, but of a "dispersed" nature, not systematic. In Canada, the Constitution Act, 1867 contains some possibilities for opting out by the provinces, and these possibilities are more numerous at the level of federal legislation establishing Canadian-wide arrangements. In Finland, there is a weak suggestion of opt out in the particular enumeration of the Parliament's powers that can be transferred to the Åland Islands by ordinary law enacted by the Parliament. The autonomy arrangement in Denmark can be considered to itself amount to a substantial opt out mechanism by means of which the Faroe Islands can, through its own decisions, transfer legislative power from the Parliament of Denmark to the Legislative Assembly of the Faroe Islands. Against this background, it is possible to conclude that the impression of rigidity in systems of double enumeration can be considerably softened by opt out mechanisms of various kinds.

The distribution of legislative powers between the national and sub-state level is not only an internal matter of the State, but has also a bearing on the relationship of the State to public international law, in particular human rights law. When sub-state legislative powers and subsequent administrative powers are exercised on persons within the sub-state entity, the sub-state entity becomes in practice the State for the purposes of international law. Yet the country itself constitutes the State which is responsible for application of international norms within the entire State in relation to other subjects of international law. If the sub-state entity exercises its legislative powers in a manner which is not consistent with the international commitments undertaken by the State, or if the concrete application of sub-state legislation by, for instance, administrative agencies of the sub-state entity violates international norms, there is little that the national government or legislature can do, because they cannot interfere by means of legislative action in the exclusive competences of the sub-state entity. Therefore, some distribution of international liability inside the State should be possible. This is not the case for Canada or Finland, where the State is responsible for the conduct of the sub-state entities, but for the Faroe Islands, the point of departure is that treaties concluded by the State of Denmark are binding unless a territorial exception has been inserted for the Faroe Islands, and that Faroese legislation that contradicts norms in international treaties is invalid.

The creation of a double enumeration of legislative powers in some countries is testimony to great legislative imagination in the law-maker which produced the fundamental norms concerning distribution of legislative powers. The practical execution of the concept of double enumerations for two different orders of government has not, however, resulted in hermetic insulation of these orders of government from each other; on the contrary, double enumeration does not normally preclude inter-governmental cooperation, but may, in fact, presuppose such cooperation and be premised on its existence. In Canada, cooperative federalism and inter-governmental cooperation has become a main mode of operation, to the extent of shifting focus from legislative federalism to executive federalism. For the Åland Islands, the Self-Government Act prescribes a host of consultative and cooperative contacts for the implementation of the legislative powers of both the Parliament of Finland and the Legislative Assembly of the Åland Islands. As concerns the Faroe Islands, the entire arrangement is based on a fundamental agreement between two entities, Denmark and the Faroe Islands, and even in other respects, negotiations between the two governments are expected to ensure the practical operation of the system. Therefore, it should not be thought that the formulation of two exclusive spheres of legislative power by means of two sets of enumerations automatically leads to detachment of the two orders of government from each other.

With the proliferation of sub-state arrangements of all sorts, both federal and autonomy arrangements, it may be useful to contemplate, as one option, the possibility of organizing the two orders of government through two enumerations of legislative powers, where the two lists are viewed as exclusive in relation to each other. Such a constitutional point of departure is, as is evidenced by our review of Canada, Denmark and Finland, completely possible and manageable, if the circumstances permit. When contemplating a system with double enumeration of legislative powers, the construction of the two lists of material contents of the enumerations is crucial, as is also the issue of how exclusive the two lists should be in relation to each other, one issue being the extent to which national supremacy or preemption is to be precluded. The more autonomy desired at the sub-state level, the less national supremacy should be permitted. This should also imply that concurrent jurisdictions explicitly formulated in the fundamental norm should be kept to a minimum.

What the level of rigidity or flexibility of the distribution of powers should be is one important consideration and turns very much on the issue of whether the distribution of power is managed by means of formal amendments, interpretation by appropriate bodies or political decisions. Here, one issue is what the arrangement should accomplish: should it separate the competences, or should it allow a cohabitation of the competences, or should it perhaps allow a re-distribution of the competences? With any distribution of legislative competence, the issue of competence control arises, and when the system is designed, there should be a determination of whether competence control is symmetrical, asymmetrical or unilateral and also whether competence control is systematic or unsystematic. Comparable issues will most certainly arise in relation to any process dealing with the creation of sub-state entities anywhere in the world or with the amendment of power distribution within such entities.

Kolibri 360 GmbH
Ferdinand-Jühlke-Straße 7
99095 Erfurt, Deutschland
produktsicherheit@kolibri360.de